SMILE OF JOY

MARY OF NAZARETH

THOMAS CASEY SJ

ISBN 978 1 9102 4897 3

Designed by Messenger Publications Design Department
Typeset in Palentino and Masqualero
Printed by Johnswood Press Ltd

Messenger Publications,
37 Lower Leeson Street, Dublin D02 W938
www.messenger.ie

To all women who have some form of 'Mary' in their names, especially my late mother Mary, my sisters Anne-Marie and Michelle Mary and my nieces Rachel Louise Mary-Clare and Rebecca Maria.

ACKNOWLEDGEMENTS

A thousand thanks to my brother Paul for reading this script in such a kind and professional manner, and for his valuable suggestions and corrections. Thank you to Fr Donal Neary of Messenger Publications for inviting me to write this book, and for his help in seeing it through to publication, as well as to Cecilia West, publisher, for her assistance; to Fr Mark-David Janus, President of Paulist Press for his strong support of this project, and to Paul McMahon of the Paulist editorial team for his helpful comments and observations.

As for the Jewish woman from Nazareth whose smile has lit up my whole life, there are no words in English – or any language – to tell her how grateful I am. She inspired this book, she is its subject: if this woman is so marvellous, what must God be like?

TABLE OF CONTENTS

INTRODUCTION

Wavelength Of Wonder

'All of a sudden the Blessed Virgin appeared
beautiful to me, so beautiful that never had I
seen anything so beautiful. Her face radiated
an indescribable kindness and love but what
penetrated to the very depths of my being was the
ravishing smile of the Blessed Virgin.'
St Thérèse of Lisieux, *The Story of a Soul*

It is amazing to think that the first smile Jesus ever gave was
in response to Mary's. Day after day Mary smiled at him,
made eye contact and spoke with those special words, those
'oohs' and 'aahs' that mothers use to communicate with
their infant children. And then one day she was graced with
the smile of Jesus in return. It must have been an extraordinary moment: her son was smiling at her, and it was God
smiling at her too. Although in the Latin language 'infant'
means speechless, Jesus was in fact already communicating,
albeit in a non-verbal way, with his first smile. And if we
could have seen that first smile of his subtitled, we would
probably have seen something like this: 'thank you for your
love, I love you too.'

This book looks at Mary, the extraordinary woman who
is 'the cause of our joy'. She is the cause of our joy because
she brought us the greatest joy of all: Jesus. She was full of
joy because she was full of gratitude, gladly acknowledging
the fullness of grace that God had given her. Her deep joy
overflowed when she visited her cousin Elizabeth: 'my soul
magnifies the Lord, and my spirit exults in God my Saviour.'

But this Magnificat song (the Latin word 'magnifies' gives this hymn of praise its name) wasn't just a once-off song of praise: the reason it came to Mary's lips so easily was because it was her usual way of praying. She constantly thanked God for the gifts he had given her. In fact, this spirit of gratitude was the secret of Mary's joy. Whatever the circumstances, Mary had the deep inner conviction that 'all shall be well, and all manner of thing shall be well' as Julian of Norwich was later to express it.

Many of us seek joy outside of ourselves, in food and drink, or in riches and reputation. Mary found an inner joy that came from encountering God, a joy that was immeasurably greater than any material joy: 'You have put into my heart a greater joy than they have from abundance of corn and new wine' *(Ps.4:8)*. By giving Mary a place in our hearts, we can find true joy in God as well.

Joy is something deeper than an artificial smile or a forced grin, and in fact a cheery expression that is permanently fixed on the face suggests superficiality. Mary's joy was not something superficial because it was above all an internal joy, as all true joy is. Mary lived in joy because she was in tune with God. If we can't experience God as joy, we're in tune with something much less than God. The only God who is believable is the God who wakens us into wonder, the wonder of joy.

Often considered the founder of modern atheism, German philosopher Friedrich Nietzsche wrote the following about Christians in *Thus Spoke Zarathustra*: 'They would have to sing better songs for me to learn to have faith in their Redeemer; and his disciples would have to look more redeemed.'

Mary had a better song, the Magnificat, which we'll reflect upon during the course of this book. It came from a deep wellspring of love inside her. It isn't so much a catchy song as a song that shows how she was gladly caught by

God. It's a song that has moved people down through the ages, because it is neither watered down nor superficial but a heartfelt cry from someone who really knows God. The joy it expresses does not involve an escape from reality, it isn't some sort of quick fix. Instead, its joy is grounded in the deep and serene confidence of Mary; a confidence that was strong enough to withstand trials and sorrows.

In reading this book, we must keep in mind that Mary entered zones of suffering that most people can't even envisage. As Jesus died his agonising death, most of his disciples had fled out of fright and bewilderment. Mary stood next to Jesus, surrounded by sneering voices that ridiculed all her hopes: 'Likewise the chief priests, elders and scribes mocked him saying, "he saved others but he cannot save himself"' (*Mt.27:41–42*).

To explore the joy of Mary and the Mary of joy, I'll follow what the New Testament tells us about her. Within the New Testament, Mary is mentioned by name in the Gospels of Matthew, Mark and Luke, as well as in the Acts of the Apostles. Although she is not actually named in the Gospel of John, it refers to her in various ways: as 'woman', 'mother' and 'mother of Jesus'. In the Book of Revelation, Mary appears in a symbolic and mysterious guise. I'll draw on these particular New Testament books to piece together her story. The first chapter introduces this childlike (not childish!) woman from Nazareth. The second chapter looks at Mary's 'yes' to becoming the mother of Jesus. The following chapters accompany Mary on her journey with Jesus, culminating in the tenth chapter, when she says her painful 'yes' to giving him back to the Father on Calvary. Then, in the second last chapter, we join Mary and the apostles as they pray for the descent of the Holy Spirit. In the final chapter, we turn to the vision of the woman clothed with the sun from the Book of Revelation. Apart from the Annunciation, the Visitation and her symbolic appearance in the Book of

Revelation, the references to Mary in the New Testament are for the most part fleeting. Yet, because all these mentions of Mary, whether brief or extended, occur in Sacred Scripture, they surge from a deep well of living water, since the Bible is written under the inspiration of the Holy Spirit. We can approach this well of salvation with joy, drawing gratefully from the infinite reservoir of God, so that like Mary we too may give thanks to the Lord, call upon his name proclaiming the wonders of him who has ushered us into his marvellous light.

The kind of Mary you'll encounter in these pages is someone who is full of God, and not of herself, someone who made God's dream her own. Mary said an enormous 'yes' to God. It was only when God's son took on human flesh that our salvation became possible. But it was only because Mary said 'yes' that God's son could take on flesh in the first place. God would never have forced a pregnancy upon Mary. Gladly for us, she gave her free and full assent.

Faith is our human 'yes' in response to God's divine 'yes' – just like a child's smile is a reply to its mother's. God gives his 'yes' first, and faith is our 'yes' in answer to his initial 'yes'. The 'yes of God is so massive we cannot imagine its vastness. God's 'yes' is utterly reliable, and complete beyond any human completeness. Our's is hesitant, fluctuating and incomplete. God's 'yes' is huge, while our's is small. God's 'yes' is eternal and stable, while our 'yes' flickers on and off. God's 'yes' is embodied in Jesus, while our's often lacks bite and reality. But as we grow spiritually, we hope that we can live our 'yes' more and more out of God's strength.

The writer Brian Moore, who grew up in a Catholic family in Belfast, began one of his short stories like this: 'In the beginning was the word and the word was No'. It's a humourous way to express the uptight and repressive side of religion.

When it comes to faith, certain Catholics feel they have

heard no too many times. That's one reason why Mary is so refreshing: she says yes.

Mary's 'yes' was strong with God's strength. After all, while the prospect of motherhood is daunting on its own, the prospect of being the mother of God is completely overwhelming. Although Mary was a human being as we are, her 'yes' nevertheless mirrored God's in a way that no one else has ever managed to do. That's because her 'yes' was filled with grace. She knew she was loved infinitely by God, and this gave her a joy that was strong enough to withstand anything that came her way.

Yet, there was nothing unreal or ethereal about Mary's 'yes'. On the contrary, it was completely real and really complete. There was nothing routine about Mary's 'yes'; it shifted the whole axis of her world and turned her life completely around. It was truly revolutionary. She had to give birth to Jesus in a poor stable on the outskirts of a village that was not her own. Together with Joseph, she had to take her new born child and flee into Egypt to escape the murderous clutches of Herod, and had no option but to remain in exile until Herod's death. She suffered the pain of widowhood after the death of her dearly beloved husband. She shared in the Passion of her son, feeling for him in his physical sufferings and in the indescribable anguish of his soul. While most of his closest disciples fled, Mary stood by the cross until the end.

Through all these difficult challenges, Mary did not waver. She had huge confidence in God. She always trusted that God would stand by her through thick and thin. When you come to think about it, a woman who is daring enough to believe that God will be born through her won't baulk at believing most anything else.

Astounding as Mary's 'yes' was, God wants something more: he wants our 'yes' as well. Because of Mary's 'yes', the word took flesh in her body. The word wants to take flesh i·

our lives also. Mary asked how the wonder of God's coming could possibly unfold within her. The angel replied that she would conceive and bear God's son through the mysterious power of the Holy Spirit. It is the same Holy Spirit who is infinitely eager to form Jesus within each of us. God created the world through the first 'yes'; Mary led the way to the redemption of the world through her's; and we, who are living in the age of the Spirit, are invited to become more godlike through uttering our own.

Even though none of us can make sense of the utter mystery that God is, at least by saying a full-blooded 'yes' we will uncover neglected layers of our own humanity, and discover that this ever-mysterious God is already present and at work within. The welcome surprise of this discovery may just inspire us with something like the grateful trust that Mary had, and which kept her always open to God's unexpected ways.

Mary, please ask God to give me true joy. I don't want to live with resentment, and I'm fed up disguising a bitter heart with a fake smile. Ask God to give me the peace that comes from doing what is right, and the serenity that comes from acting as he wants me to act, so that I can have true joy as you did. The kind of joy that no adversity is strong enough to destroy.

CHAPTER 1

Girl From Galilee

'The eyes of Our Lady are... eyes of gentle
compassion... and with a kind of feeling in them
that cannot be described, which is beyond concepts
and words, something that makes her younger than
sin, younger than the race from which she sprang,
and though a Mother by grace, indeed Mother of
graces, yet at the same time the youngest
sister of humankind.'
Georges Bernanos, *The Diary of a Country Priest*

In Hebrew, the sacred language of the Jewish faith, and in
Aramaic, the once spoken language of Palestine, Mary's
name was Miryam. Perhaps her name is linked with the
Egyptian word 'mery', meaning beloved or cherished, or
it could be connected with the Hebrew words 'bitter' (*mar*)
and 'sea' (*yam*). Indeed, a German academic once wrote a
book in which he explored seventy possible meanings for
Mary's name! Although scholars offer many different expla-
nations for her name, many saints link her name in one way
or another with the 'sea'. For the fourth-century St Jerome,
God was like the sea, and Mary was a drop in this infinite
ocean. St Jerome apparently called Mary *Stilla Maris*, or
'drop of the sea'. But because of a copyist's error, one single
letter was changed, and as a result this phrase became *Stella
Maris*, or 'star of the sea'. Over time, 'Star of the Sea' became
one of the most beloved ways of describing Mary, because
so many devout people experienced her as a light guiding
them through the storms and tempests of life until the

could safely reach port. Saints also described her as a 'bitter sea', because of the immense sufferings she endured on account of her compassion for her son. Even though there is a whole 'sea' of meanings when it comes to Mary's name, the Egyptian word for beloved and the Hebrew word for bitter already tell us something of Mary's unique destiny: especially beloved by God, and yet destined to undergo the unspeakable sorrow of seeing her only son, who was also the Son of God, dying on the cross. The special place that Mary has held through the centuries in Irish hearts is shown by the fact that in the Irish language, she is the only Mary called 'Muire'. Every other Mary is 'Máire'.

Mary was a Jewish woman. She would have spoken Aramaic. She would have heard Hebrew as the Torah was read out in the synagogue, and most likely she would have also read the Hebrew Scriptures herself. She was a cousin of Elizabeth, the wife of the priest Zechariah, and mother of John the Baptist. Not only was Elizabeth's own husband a priest but Elizabeth herself was 'a descendant of Aaron' *(Lk.1:5)*, the first in Israel's long line of priests, and the brother of Moses. It makes sense that Elizabeth's cousin Mary would have been brought up in a highly religious atmosphere too. In the apocryphal gospel of James, the names of Mary's parents are given as Joachim and Anne, and Joachim is portrayed as a wealthy and devout man who gave generously to the poor. It's also interesting to note that Elizabeth was the name of the wife of the first high priest, Moses' brother Aaron; and to recall that Mary shared the same name as the sister of Moses and Aaron, the name 'Miriam'.

Mary lived in Galilee, an obscure corner of a little-known 'nce of the Roman Empire. She didn't live in one of the 'us towns along the Sea of Galilee but in the simple 'zareth, set among its rolling hills. In fact, Naza- 'n uneventful little place that a man called Na- identified with the apostle Bartholomew) couldn't imagine anything worthwhile emerging from it at all: 'Can anything good come out of Nazareth?' *(Jn.1:46).*

Mary had a happiness that wasn't based on outward things. Just as well, because if Nathanael was correct, Nazareth hadn't much to offer. So what gave her joy? She was convinced that she was loved infinitely by God. She knew that God was her shepherd and guide, but not a merely external guide for she also felt God's presence deep within her. And this presence of God was an active presence: she was certain that God was at work in her heart. She was sure that God was making everything work together not only for her good but also for the good of her people, Israel. Even though life was ordinary in Nazareth, she sensed that something extraordinary was on the way. She felt that a sunrise of wonder was about to bless the life of her people, and draw them out of their tiny lives into a bigger story, the inbreaking story of the Messiah.

You have to be a child to have the lightness of heart to believe in wonder, to trust that your life is made for a big story and to have confidence in the master storyteller who is at work behind the scenes. And, in the very best sense of the word, Mary was a child: she never grew up. As the French novelist Georges Bernanos memorably wrote, this extraordinary woman stayed so young that she was 'younger than sin' because she was innocence itself.

Somebody might object that everyone sins, or as St Paul said, 'all have sinned' *(Rom.3:23).* But isn't a child of three weeks or three months or three years too young to sin? Mary was that kind of innocent child, and what's more, she retained that extraordinary childhood innocence her whole life long, which is why she is younger than sin.

But if Mary is innocence itself, how could she have said 'my spirit rejoices in God my Saviour' *(Lk.1:47)?* How could she have been saved by the Saviour if she hadn't been lost in the first place? Here's a way of approaching this mystery:

just imagine you're walking in a park on a summer's day when you see a baby dove trying to fly for the first time. It lands awkwardly near a large pond of water, and you realise that since it cannot get a foothold on the slippery stones leading down to the pond, it is in danger of falling into the water. You pick up the tiny creature and save it before it falls into danger. In other words, you save it before things go wrong, and not afterwards. That's what God did with Mary, and that's why she was so full of joy and gratitude toward her Saviour. Another way of appreciating what God did for Mary is to take an analogy from preventive medicine. We know that doctors can successfully treat patients who are ill, and even seriously ill. However, doctors can also 'cure' people in advance by advising them to take preventive measures. For instance, a doctor may advise a woman to reduce her consumption of alcohol, nicotine or even sugar during pregnancy in order to save her child from being born with certain illnesses or defects. Mary too was saved in advance, in the womb, by not inheriting original sin and its consequences in the first place.

Mary always remained a child, totally dependent upon God, gladly receiving everything from God's hands, and never wanting to be apart from him. Mary's spirit is the spirit of childhood, a combination of utter powerlessness and immense confidence. A child is small and helpless, yet isn't closed in on itself but delights in the world around it, full of a sense of wonder and trust. A child walks along the road of life with a spirit of astonishment, and with enough confidence to believe that God may appear at any turn. Mary looked at the path of life with the eyes of a child.

We could all gain a lot by recovering this spirit of childhood, by becoming again faithful to the children we once were. One of Pope Francis' favourite poems puts this well. It is by Friedrich Hölderlin, and is dedicated to his grandmother. It finishes with the line; 'May the man hold fast to what the child has promised.' The child is filled with hope because it sees beauty everywhere, a beauty that is invisible to sceptics and cynics. Mary had that childlike spirit, that transparency and that simplicity, because she surrendered herself completely to God.

With her childlike nature, Mary was truly little and she gladly acknowledged it. She was totally dependent upon God, she gave herself fully to him and she sought to serve God as he wished to be served. It was because of this extraordinary humility that through her Christ became one of us, in the process making Mary rich in God.

Mary, I'd like to give myself more fully to God but at the same time I'm nervous about doing so. I'd like to be able to say a full 'yes', but all I can manage for now is something partial. Maybe we could pray this prayer of St Ignatius of Loyola together regularly, so that some of your sublime self-giving will rub off on me, and then one day I'll be able to say it with something approaching your integrity:
'Take Lord receive, all my liberty,
My memory, my understanding, my entire will.
Give me only your love and your grace.
These are enough for me.'

CHAPTER 2

Gladness Of Grace

'I don't know who – or what – put the question, I
don't know when it was put. I don't even remember
answering. But at some moment I did answer "yes"
to someone – or something – and from that hour I
was certain that existence is meaningful and that,
therefore, my life, in self-surrender, had a goal.'
Dag Hammarskjöld, *Markings*

Mary became engaged to a carpenter named Joseph. In that
era, it was usual for Jewish girls to become engaged at the
age of thirteen. At this moment in her life, when she was just
a young teenager, solidly connected with a man to whom
she was promised in marriage, something extraordinary un-
folded. Shortly after the engagement, the angel Gabriel visited her. His first word of greeting was an invitation to joy:
Gabriel said 'Rejoice' *(Lk.1:28)*. He then proceeded to give
Mary a new name! He called Mary 'the one who has always
been full of grace' *(Lk.1:28)*, which is even more striking
than the familiar phrase we use: 'full of grace'. This was the
first title Mary ever received. Long before the Church started giving Mary her many titles, God, through his messenger Gabriel, had already bestowed this title upon her. Notice
that the emphasis isn't on Mary or on her virtues or merits.
The phrase 'the one who has always been full of grace' tells
us what God has done for Mary. God has poured his love
into Mary's heart, and it is this love of God that makes her
worthy, not anything she has done herself. All that she is
and all that she has – everything is God's gift to her.

Grace comes into our lives when God turns toward us with his love that we don't deserve, yet which floods our hearts, draws us toward him and makes us sharers in his divine life. That's how it happened for Mary as well. Grace ushered Mary into a wonderful world where she could relate to God as the most intimate of friends. Grace raised her up, making it possible for her to love in a way she could never have loved by herself.

Grace and joy are closely related in life: when anyone treats us graciously or favourably, we experience joy. Grace and joy are closely connected in the New Testament as well. In fact the words look really similar in the Greek language in which the New Testament was written: 'grace' is *charis*, and 'joy' is *chara* (and by the way, the first word of the Angel Gabriel's greeting – 'rejoice' – was another closely connected word: *'chaire'*). The similarity between grace and joy is in more than the spelling, because when grace enters someone's life, joy accompanies it. Mary's deep joy wasn't something she produced herself; its origin was divine. This joy wasn't dependent upon outward circumstances, because it was the fruit of the Holy Spirit. Grace didn't bring Mary a momentary thrill but lasting joy. Grace didn't bring Mary surface glee but inner delight.

The words of the angel Gabriel are often translated as 'full of grace'. Impressive as the words 'full of grace' are, they are still not powerful enough to express what the angel Gabriel was really saying to Mary. That's why I use the expression 'the one who has always been full of grace'.

In the Acts of the Apostles, we're told that Stephen, the first Christian martyr, was a man 'full of grace' (*pleres charistos*). Although this means that Stephen was filled with grace at a given moment in time, it doesn't mean that he had always been filled with grace. The angel Gabriel used a significantly different term when he greeted Mary: the word *'kecharitomene'*. This word does not appear elsewhere in the Bible. In fact, it does not appear anywhere else in all of Greek literature. It is a once-off word for a one-of-a-kind woman. The word 'kecharitomene' means fully and flawlessly filled with grace. It doesn't merely mean that someone is filled with grace just for now or only in the present moment. It means that someone, although filled with grace in the past, still continues to be filled with that same grace in the present, in such a complete way that they will most likely always be full of grace. It's a word for someone who has permanent and perfect grace.

This wonderful word implies that Mary was full of amazing grace from the very beginning. For the rest of us, our closeness, communion and fellowship with God are given at baptism. But in Mary's case, this gift of intimacy and communion with God was given to her from the moment her life began in the womb. And God's grace enabled her to continue living like that her whole life through. This privilege was given by God: just as in the case of Adam and Eve, God created Mary without original sin. The word 'kecharitomene' already hints at the Immaculate Conception. Or to put it in a different way, this compelling Greek word is the first glimpse of what would later be clearly expressed in the belief 'that the Blessed Virgin Mary, at the first instant of her conception, by a singular privilege and grace of the omnipotent God, in virtue of the merits of Jesus Christ, the Saviour of mankind, was preserved immaculate from all stain of original sin' (Pope Pius IX).

The heart warming news is that we're all invited to share in the Immaculate Conception. It's not just Mary's privilege – it's a privilege open to everyone. Certainly, Mary received it in a matchless way, she was filled with the Holy Spirit from the moment of her conception. Even though our life is already well underway, we can receive this gift as well. In fact, there was someone soon after Mary who received the Holy Spirit in his mother's womb: John the Baptist. Although we're no longer in the womb, God can still make of us what he has always wanted us to be. This is really what St Paul is getting at in the Letter to the Ephesians (*Eph.1:4*), when he emphasises that even before God created the world, he had already chosen us in Christ to be holy and without fault in his sight.

Grace is not some inert thing but God himself, giving us the gift of his life and love. Even if we've never had this gift, we can still receive it. The Immaculate Conception means that Mary was saved, and saved in advance. However, Mary is not the only one who can be saved. We are all offered salvation. God wants to privilege each one of us, and he doesn't want to wait until some vague point in the remote future to do so. He wants to give each of us the fullness of grace as soon as possible. Note the present tense in Mary's description of herself to Bernadette Soubirous in the grotto of Massabielle in 1858: 'I am the Immaculate Conception'. Mary didn't say 'I was immaculately conceived'. That's because the grace of the Immaculate Conception is not just a past reality but instead something that is active and at work in the present moment. It's something we can access in the here and now of our lives. By looking at Mary we come to realise that this marvellous gift is available to us as well: she is the reason for our hope.

The Immaculate Conception means that Mary was always in a fully healthy relationship with God. God wants to usher each of us into a right relationship with him. God wants to give us the light and the fire of the Holy Spirit. God wants to surround us with grace. God wants to save us in the most radical and generous way possible. The following words, attributed to Pedro Arrupe, the inspirational twentieth century Basque Jesuit, convey in an eloquent manner what it means to be wholly taken up by God, to become an 'Immaculate Conception' so to speak: 'Nothing is more practical than finding God, than falling in love in a quite absolute, final way. What you are in love with, what seizes your imagination, will affect everything. It will decide what will get you out of bed in the morning, what you do with your evenings, how you spend your weekends, what you read, whom you know, what breaks your heart, and what amazes you with joy and gratitude. Fall in love, stay in love, and it will decide everything.'

For all the wonder of those words, the gift of the Immaculate Conception won't wave a magic wand over our lives, suddenly exempting us from the griefs and pains that are part of the human condition. If we receive the gift of the Immaculate Conception as Mary did, the normal experiences of life will continue as before: although we'll have moments of profound joy, we won't be spared the inevitable struggles and difficulties of life. There will be one crucial difference, however: the problems we encounter won't cause the same inner turbulence they once did. That's because we'll have fallen in love with God, and his sheer presence will be sufficient to calm our worst fears. We'll be blessed with a deep-down peace, the kind of peace that enables us to deal serenely with the annoyances and aggravations of our scattered lives.

With this special word, *kecharitomene*, Gabriel was naming the sheer abundance of grace that had always flooded Mary's heart and always would. He was highlighting the fact that she was gifted in an astonishing way. Just like someone might call the world's best soccer player, 'Mr Soccer', the angel Gabriel was effectively calling Mary 'Ms. Grace'. He was effectively saying: 'you have always been fully and perfectly filled with grace and you always will. .' This was a way of underlining her utter uniqueness. Because she was unique, she had a unique name, a name given her by heaven. Anyone given a special mission by God is given a special name, like Simon, who was called Peter, meaning 'rock'. Mary's mission was to give birth to the one who was holy beyond words, and the Most High had to come forth from the most grace-filled person of all, the *kecharitomene*, the one always filled with grace.

The angel Gabriel then said to Mary: 'The Lord is with you' *(Lk.1:28)*. In the Book of Judges *(Judg.6:12)*, the same words were uttered by an angel to the young man Gideon, when he was given the mission to serve his people as a warrior, a leader and a man of faith. Mary too was called to serve God's people in a vital way, and so the angel assured her that God was at her side, and that she could rely on his powerful support.

This expression of God's closeness and help was intended to reassure Mary. Yet, reassurance didn't come immediately because Mary was puzzled, asking herself what the angel Gabriel's greeting could possibly mean. There was probably a struggle going on inside her between the angel's words of affirmation and her own humility. God wanted to raise Mary up even more, yet all Mary wanted to do was to humble herself before God. Mary was so humble that she wasn't aware of her own greatness. Yet, despite the internal struggle caused by the angel's words, she remained calm and collected. Most of us would be so overcome by the sudden arrival of a heavenly messenger that we wouldn't be able to think straight. Although Mary was perplexed by the angel's greeting, she didn't lose her sense of peace. She was a reflective woman and questioned herself about the meaning of his message. This episode shows us that Mary was a reflective woman, and that the spirit of reflection has always been a vital aspect of Christian life. As soon as she heard the words of the angel, Mary was already pondering their meaning.

Because Gabriel was inspired by God, he knew the concerns that preoccupied her. He calmed her by saying, 'Do not be afraid, Mary, for you have found favour with God' *(Lk.1:30)*. He then went on to explain that God wanted her to conceive a son who would be called Jesus, and who would be the Son of the Most High. The angel Gabriel was asking her to make a huge shift in her way of life. She was being asked to take on the enormous responsibility of giving all of herself to this special child. Not just for the nine months this unique child would be in her womb but for always. Becoming a mother would open up a new and unexpected path. There would be no life for her apart from this child, because the child's interests would be at the very core of her own. Everything she was to do would be driven by the desire to do the best possible for her son.

There was still one important issue that Mary needed to resolve: 'How can this be, since I am a virgin?' *(Lk.1:34)* Mary was completely given to God. She had made a total commitment of herself to God (otherwise her question wouldn't have made sense). Evidently she must have told Joseph about this commitment when they became engaged, and he was at peace with her decision. She wanted to be a flower that only bloomed in God's sight, and she presumed that in order to give birth to this child she would first have to enter into intimate relations with Joseph, thus compromising her total self-giving to God. And that was something she did not feel comfortable with, because all she wanted was that every thought of hers would be a thought for God. She wanted to have eyes only for him, ears only to listen to his voice, lips to sing only his praise. She was worried that this new mission might stop her from belonging completely to God, from being 'a garden locked, a fountain sealed' *(Song.4:12)*.

Again, the angel answered her core concern: 'The Holy Spirit will come upon you, and the power of the Most High will overshadow you' *(Lk.1:35)*. The angel made it clear that Joseph, the man to whom Mary was engaged, would have no part to play in the conception of this child. All Mary needed to do was to give her assent, and then God's own creative power would bring this child into existence. Because this child would be the gift of God, and not of any man, the angel Gabriel emphasised that 'the child to be born will be holy; he will be called the Son of God' *(Lk.1:35)*. Son of God because the Son of the Heavenly Father, and not of any earthly father. Mary's unique relationship with God would not be compromised.

We are so familiar with the story of the Annunciation, that it can be easy to take Mary's faith for granted. It's easy to forget that Gabriel's message opened up a vast new horizon for Mary. He didn't give Mary any human guarantees, he didn't offer her a familiar or secure way forward. He took her completely beyond any comfort zone. Everything about this singular episode demanded a huge leap of faith: it was already hard enough to accept that an angel was speaking to her, it was even more difficult to believe that a virgin could conceive but who could imagine that any woman could possibly become God's own mother! Gabriel was painting a picture that bordered on the preposterous. Mary didn't stop to think about the sheer unlikelihood of what was being announced. If she had, she would most likely have refused to believe. Mary's focus was on God. She believed enough in God's power and love to accept the message that Gabriel communicated to her. She plunged wholeheartedly into the limitless ocean of God as she said: 'behold the servant of the Lord, let it be done unto me according to your word' *(Lk.1:38)*.

This phrase 'let it be done' can give the wrong impression. It can imply that Mary was only passively accepting what God asked of her. In truth, what Mary expressed in the original Greek of the New Testament was a joyful longing to make God's wishes her own. The noted Jesuit scriptural scholar Ignace de la Potterie explains that in Greek, Mary's *fiat* (the succinct way of saying 'let it be done' in Latin): 'expresses "a joyous desire to" never a resignation or a constraining submission before something burdensome and painful... The *fiat* of Mary is not just a simple acceptance and even less, a resignation. It is rather a joyous desire to collaborate with what God foresees for her. It is the joy of total abandonment to the good will of God.'

Since God was about to humble himself to the utmost by becoming one of us, he wanted to find the utmost humility in the one through whom he took on our flesh. Mary's humility – 'behold the servant of the Lord' – stands out because it is joined to complete goodness: the angel saluted her as 'the one who has always been full of grace'. If someone has nothing to boast about, they're necessarily humble. If someone has something going for them, their humility is something to be admired. If someone has everything going for them – if they're permanently and perfectly full of grace – their humility is nothing short of miraculous. And the miracle of Mary's humility was necessary for the Incarnation.

Just stop to think about it: an angel was sent by God to this young Jewish teenager. He told Mary that she was and always had been full of grace, that she had found God's favour and that she would conceive a son called Jesus who would be the Son of the Most High, who would be given the throne of David, who would reign over the house of Jacob forever and whose kingdom would have no end. He also told her that the Holy Spirit would come upon her, and that her child would be the Son of God. Could the angel have told her anything more marvellous? And since he made these astonishing promises, wouldn't it have been understandable if she began to have a high opinion of herself, especially because the words of Gabriel weren't mere flattery but the truth, since these words were from God?

The angel Gabriel told her all this, he told her she was to be the mother of God and Mary responded by describing herself as God's servant. This self-description typifies her whole attitude. She did not think: 'now everyone will look up to me, because I am about to become like God, creating the human flesh of God.' On the contrary, she lowered herself even more, calling herself a servant, just like her son, who 'emptied himself, taking the form of a servant' *(Phil.2:7)*. Rather than assuming the title 'mother', which might have led to thoughts of superiority, Mary called herself a servant to reaffirm her dependence upon God, and her complete surrender to him.

Although Mary was filled with God's grace, she also needed to be empty of herself in order to receive God's son. If she had been full of herself, there would have been no space left in her heart for God. Humility carved out this welcoming emptiness inside her, which made it possible for her to become a container containing the uncontainable.

Pope Francis observed that 'every "yes" to God gives rise to stories of salvation for us and for others. Like Mary with her own "yes"' (8 December 2016). Humble as Mary's 'yes' to the angel Gabriel was, it gave rise to a huge story of freedom for us. What's more, the daring and confidence of Mary's 'yes' mirrored God's massive 'yes' in creating us. The first 'yes' was God's, God's 'Let there be light' *(Gen.1:3)*. The whole of creation poured forth from these powerful words, galaxy upon galaxy, countless stars scattered across the vast reaches of space like necklaces of pearls, then planet after planet, and finally human life itself. And when the fullness of time came, Mary echoed God's 'yes' in her 'Let it be done unto me according to thy Word' *(Lk.1:38)*. Because of Mary's 'yes', God was able to take on human flesh. God becoming one of us: that's the most amazing thing that has ever happened in the history of the world. God became one of us so that through the miracle of grace we could partake in his divine nature. And when the angel Gabriel asked Mary to conceive, bear a son and name him Jesus, the world, paradise, and the Heavenly Father himself were all on tenterhooks awaiting her response. Even though God knew she would say 'yes', because he knew her every thought and action, this advance knowledge did not force Mary's consent. As St Augustine once put it: 'Just as your memory does not force the past to have happened, God's foreknowledge does not force the future to happen.' Being already and perennially full of grace, Mary was certainly accustomed to saying 'yes' to God. But she was still free. God was reaching out to her at that moment with colossal hope. Mary said 'let it be'. The German Jesuit theologian Karl Rahner remarked: 'In an instant that will exist for all time and remain for all eternity, Mary's word was the word of humankind and her "yes" was the Amen of all creation to God's "yes".' What happened as a result was breathtaking. To quote Karl Rahner again: 'When we say, "It is Christmas," we mean that God has spoken into the world his last, his deepest, his most beautiful word in the incarnate Word... And this word means: I love you, you, the world and humankind.' But before the Father uttered his splendid 'yes' to the world in the birth of Jesus, he wanted to hear Mary's own 'yes'.

Even though everyone didn't welcome Jesus with open arms, there was at least one human being who received him in a fitting way on behalf of us all – and that person was Mary. She didn't merely receive her Lord in a passive or resigned manner. She opened her whole being to the gift of God's love in the promise of Jesus. That's why before she ever conceived Jesus in her womb, she had already conceived him in her heart.

The angel Gabriel told Mary that her elderly cousin Elizabeth, said to be barren, had defied all expectations, and was now six months pregnant. Mary immediately made a long journey to the mountainous country near Jerusalem in order to visit Elizabeth and be of help to her. Because this journey took several days, Mary had the opportunity to reflect on the monumental news she had just received from the angel Gabriel. She began to take in some of its mind-boggling richness. Mary felt huge joy in her heart, and at the same time deep reverence, because the God within her was the infinite and holy one, the one in whose presence Moses had removed the very shoes from his feet. And this God was now coming into the world through her, his lowly servant. For now this news was secret, yet Mary wanted to share it with the people around her, because she knew this was a secret that could bring them the happiness for which they longed. All around her were people who experienced griefs as well as joys, struggles as well as moments of elation. Mary wanted to tell them that love was coming into the world. Deep down we all hope that behind the ups and downs of life, behind the little tragedies and the big ones, there is love. And all around Mary were people who longed for the Messiah and for a new era where justice and peace would reign. Mary wanted to tell them that love was coming into the world but because she knew that God's secrets are sacred, she remained silent. Everything that had happened so far was because of God's initiative, and so Mary also entrusted to God the task of sharing this message as and when he chose. God had already decided who would be the first person apart from Mary to become privy to this wondrous story: it was to be Mary's own cousin Elizabeth.

O God of 'yes', your love for me sounds so simple, so soft,
that sometimes I don't realize how marvellous it is.
Speak to me in words that are new and different
about this love you have for me.
And please be patient with my hesitations.
I want to say 'yes', but so often I say 'maybe' or 'I'm not ready'.
Help me to go beyond these ifs and buts.
May the Spirit help me to breathe in fresh possibilities,
and go beyond my shivering indecision to a
'yes' like Mary's, so full and free that it's
like something I'm saying for the first time.

CHAPTER 3

Prayer Of Praise

'The proud cannot bring themselves to hold out
empty hands to God, they insist on offering virtues,
good works, self denials, anything in order not to
have nothing. They want to be beautiful for him
from their own resources, whereas we are beautiful
only because God looks on us and makes us
beautiful. This is repugnant to pride. God cannot
give himself to us unless our hands are empty to
receive him. The deepest reason why so few of us
are saints is because we will not let God love us.
To be loved means a naked, defenceless surrender
to all God is. It means a glad acceptance of our
nothingness, a look fixed only on the God who
gives, taking no account of the nothing to whom the
gift is made.'
Ruth Burrows, *Guidelines for Mystical Prayer*

Two women, both carrying children, both joyous that God
had intervened so miraculously in their lives and both empty enough of themselves to be filled with the Holy Spirit:
that's the wonder of Mary's encounter with Elizabeth.

We often think that being holy means doing spectacular
or dramatic things. Yet, when Mary arrives at Elizabeth's
door she is doing what countless women have no doubt
done throughout history: she is visiting her cousin. Doing
extraordinary things is not necessary for holiness; what is
necessary is doing ordinary things with a big heart. As Jean-
Pierre de Caussade, the eighteenth century French Jesuit

priest, said: 'It is the heart that must be changed. When I say heart, I mean will. Sanctity, then, consists in willing all that God wills for us. Yes! Sanctity of heart is a simple '*fiat*', a conformity of will with the will of God.' This was Mary's secret: she made God's will her own. The angel Gabriel told her about Elizabeth's pregnancy, and Mary knew that her aging cousin would need her help at this crucial point in her life: that was enough incentive for her to undertake this long journey. Mary shaped everything around God, and not around herself. She didn't take on God's will in a mournful or begrudging manner; she embraced it with joy and gratitude. She didn't just accept it in a passive way; she actively made it her own. And God loves nothing more than a cheerful giver.

Things hadn't been easy in Elizabeth's house: although she had experienced the marvellous joy of conceiving a child, her husband Zechariah had been struck dumb for not believing the words of the angel Gabriel. He remained mute until shortly after their son's birth. After so many years of marriage, after so many deep and heartfelt conversations together, now there was only silence from Zechariah. His expression was pained and awkward. For Zechariah, this trial of silence was also a strange blessing: it gave him time to absorb this astounding news, and to deepen his sense of reverence and gratitude. For Elizabeth things were different. It was precisely now that she would have loved to converse with him at length about what was to take place. Just like Elizabeth, Zechariah was 'righteous before God' *(Lk.1:6)*, and he was also a priest, so he was accustomed to interpreting and teaching the Scriptures. At this special moment in her life, hearing the consoling words of Scripture from her husband would have been of enormous support to Elizabeth. She needed someone to listen to her, someone who could understand her unique situation.

That someone arrived when Elizabeth received the special

grace of a three-month-long visit from her cousin Mary. The Gospel of Luke is silent about the kind of greeting Mary gave Elizabeth. The Gospel does, however, describe its spectacular impact: 'When Elizabeth heard Mary's greeting, the child leapt in her womb, and Elizabeth was filled with the Holy Spirit' *(Lk.1:41)*. And a few verses later, Elizabeth herself says: 'as soon as I heard the sound of your greeting, the child in my womb leapt for joy' *(Lk.1:44)*.

The effect of Mary's greeting upon Elizabeth shows how powerful words are. Words are so creative that in the first chapter of Genesis God speaks and the world comes into being. From the dawn of creation, God has communicated with us through words. *The* word of all words is Jesus, the Word of God: 'in the beginning was the Word, and the Word was with God, and the word was God' *(Jn.1:1)*. The Prologue of John's Gospel goes on to tell us that 'through him all things were made' *(Jn.1:3)*. It is through the creative Word of God that the world comes into being. As the Letter to the Hebrews tells us: 'God...has spoken to us through the Son...through whom also he created the world' *(Heb.1:1–2)*. The unique, overflowing, and self-giving divine word is mirrored in myriad ways in our life-giving human words. Mary's greeting was a 'creative' word, raising up something new in Elizabeth's heart. It was as though Jesus, wordlessly present in her womb, were already speaking in and through Mary. This was because Mary was speaking out of the deepest layer of her own humanity where she belonged to the God who also belonged to her.

When Elizabeth heard Mary's words, she was hit with a pulse of divine energy, 'filled with the Holy Spirit'. Elizabeth spoke out of this new fullness, and so her words were full of meaning. Because of the Holy Spirit, Elizabeth was able to recognise some remarkable things about her cousin: that Mary was blessed among women, that she was carrying the Lord in her womb, and that she was a woman of immense faith. Without the help of the Holy Spirit, Elizabeth would have seen little more than an exceptionally kind and compassionate woman when she met her cousin, and even that would have already been a lot to see. Thanks to the light of the Holy Spirit, Elizabeth saw that Mary had been given unprecedented gifts by God. In fact, Elizabeth didn't call Mary her cousin at all; she called her 'the mother of my Lord' (Lk.1:43). She recognided that there was something qualitatively different about Mary: this was no longer her devout young cousin but the most saintly woman she could possibly encounter.

The Holy Spirit, who filled Elizabeth at that moment, helped her to glimpse something of the wonder of Mary. The Holy Spirit was of course also at work in Mary, 'knitting' (as Psalm 139 would put it) together the human nature of Jesus in his mother's womb. Luke's Gospel points to an intimate bond between the Holy Spirit and Mary from the moment of the Annunciation, when the Holy Spirit overshadowed her.

The creativity of the Spirit exceeded the wildest dreams of both Mary and Elizabeth. Despite their immense goodness, neither Mary nor Elizabeth could have ever anticipated a moment like this – young virgins and old sterile women simply don't give birth! Thanks to God's grace, these two women, related by blood and by a shared longing for God, were both on the way to bringing new life into the world.

Filled with the Holy Spirit, Elizabeth said to Mary 'blessed are you among women' (Lk.1:42). The Greek word used by Elizabeth here, eulogetos, is the root of the English word 'eulogy', a speech in which someone is highly praised. And the word 'blessed' as used here by Elizabeth, means something similar: it means that someone is highly thought of and highly spoken of, with a character beyond reproach. A few verses later, Elizabeth once again called Mary blessed, saying, 'Blessed is she who believed that there would be a fulfilment of what was spoken to her by the Lord' *(Lk.1:45)*. This second time, Elizabeth used a different word for blessed, the Greek word *'makarios'*, which means blessed in a thoroughly deep and full way. It is a blessedness that doesn't get weakened by adverse circumstance but withstands the adversities of life. It is a blessedness that comes from God, from being filled with God. And it is a blessedness that, through faith, enables us to partake in God's own nature.

In response to being called 'blessed' in this profound and expansive way, Mary burst forth into praise, a praise that issued from the very depths of this blessedness and joy. Normally so quiet and self-effacing, Mary could not restrain the joy that bubbled inside. She shared her happiness with Elizabeth. Mary uttered the song of praise that we call the Magnificat. This song of praise is filled with allusions to the Old Testament. It shows how at home Mary was in the Hebrew Scriptures. The Bible was in her blood, so to speak, so much so that she could link a passage from the First Book of Samuel with a line from the Psalms; she could connect the joyful praise of the prophet Isaiah with words of rejoicing from the prophet Habakkuk. That's because she saw the Bible as a single and interconnected living organism: as the living Word of God, as 'something alive and active, cutting like any double-edged sword but more finely…able to judge the thoughts and intentions of the heart' *(Heb.4:12)*. For Mary, each verse was a gateway into other verses – and into the presence of God. She was so immersed in Scripture that the Magnificat alludes to more than a dozen different psalms, as well as to Genesis, the First and Second Book of Samuel and the prophets Isaiah, Micah and Habakkuk.

Mary's poetic outburst is a celebration of God's wonders. It's not a song about herself but about God, and in it Mary looks at God from three different angles: first, her own experience of God, second, how God relates to human beings in general and third, how God interacts with the chosen people of Israel. All the powers of Mary's soul clicked into gear as she praised God's greatness and mercy. The Venerable Bede, the English saint and doctor of he Church born in the late seventh century, offers a magnificent paraphrase of the opening words of the Magnificat. In a passage from his *Commentary on Saint Luke's Gospel* (which is the second reading in the The Office of Readings each twenty-second of December), Bede notes:

'Mary said: my soul glorifies the Lord, my spirit rejoices in God, my Saviour. The Lord has exalted me with a great and unheard of gift, which cannot be explained in any words, and can scarcely be understood by the deepest feelings of the heart. And so I offer up all the strength of my soul in thanksgiving and praise. In my joy I pour out all my life, all my feeling, all my understanding in contemplating the greatness of him who is without end. My spirit rejoices in the eternal divinity of Jesus, my Saviour, whom I have conceived in time and bear in my body.'

Mary's next words highlight humility as well as awe before God: 'for he has been mindful of the humble state of his servant' *(Lk.1:48)*. Mary describes herself as lowly because, compared with God, everyone, no matter how exalted, is lowly, and Mary was no exception. Humility is the recognition of the truth. And humility makes it possible for us to begin to see God. C.S. Lewis once commented: 'As long as you are proud you cannot know God. A proud man is always looking down on things and people: and, of course, as long as you are looking down you cannot see something that is above you.' Mary always looked up.

Mary goes on to announce that 'all generations will call me blessed' *(Lk.1:48)*. Many people seek fame during their lives; Mary, by contrast, was happy to stay unknown. Yet, while many famous people are quickly forgotten Mary knew that although she would remain obscure during her lifetime, things would be different when her earthly life came to an end. Why is it that all generations will call Mary blessed? There are many reasons: her fullness of grace, the great things the Almighty has done for her, her faith that fully responded to the gift of God's love, her blessedness among women and of course the blessed fruit of her womb. Mary was keenly aware that God had constantly been showering blessings upon her. She knew that everything was gift. Mary received God's love, and gave back love in return. Mary was alive to God's gift, joyfully giving her constant 'yes' in response. True greatness is not about what we do for God but about what we allow God to do in us, by uttering our free and full 'let it be'. Mary grasped what it means to be a human being: it means to be totally blessed, so that what we give back to God is itself God's gift: God's own love. As St Paul puts it: 'For it is God who is at work in you, both to will and to act according to his good purpose' (*Phil.2:13*).

'His mercy is for those who fear him from generation to generation' *(Lk.1:50)*. Mary places her own life within a larger horizon. Her memory is never in search only of herself; it is always in search of God, and for how God is at work in her life. Because Mary knows her own story is part of God's story, she can be confident that there is nothing random about her life. There is continuity, there is sense and there is purpose: 'The Almighty has done great things for me and holy is his name' *(Lk.1 49)*. That's why, when she has to give birth to Jesus in an abandoned stable because there's no room for them in any inn, she doesn't lose her sense of peace. With ourselves by contrast, a traffic jam, an appointment with the dentist or bad weather can often be enough to throw us off balance.

The Magnificat also shows that Mary understands the main things that prevent us from acknowledging how indebted we are to God: pride, power, pleasure and possessions. These idols distract us from our emptiness. Although the arrogant lord it over others, they will eventually be humiliated. As for those who cling to power, they will one day be stripped of their thrones. And if the rich turn their possessions into mini-gods, they will ultimately lose everything. There will be reversals that surprise us, and these dramatic turnarounds will lift up all those who place their trust in God: 'He has scattered those who are proud in their inmost thoughts. He has brought down rulers from their thrones but has lifted up the humble. He has filled the hungry with good things but has sent the rich away empty.' *(Lk.1:51–53)*. Mary's song does not tell us when these tumultuous changes will take place, and how they will unfold but Mary is sure they will happen.

As she comes to the end of her song of praise, Mary remembers God's mercy, his fidelity to the promises he has made to her people, 'to Abraham and his descendants forever' *(Lk.1:55)*. This song of praise that pours forth from her heart when she visits her cousin Elizabeth shows that she carries in her memory the whole history of God's love for her people. Mary is so rooted in remembering God's past promises that she has no doubt that God will continue to keep his amazing promises. Mary's way of remembering invites each of us to search our past for signs of God, to look for the blessings God has given us, to uncover the ways God has entered into our lives and to open up the often hidden treasures of God's goodness in the storehouse of our memory. And if we find it difficult to access these life-giving memories, we can pray for the grace of growing in gratitude.

When the Angel Gabriel told Mary that her cousin Elizabeth was six months pregnant, she set out for the house of Elizabeth and stayed there for three months. Mary would have naturally wanted to remain with her aged cousin until Elizabeth recovered her strength after the exhaustion of giving birth at such an advanced age. During those three months Mary's very presence must have been a balm for Elizabeth. Just to look at her young cousin's caressing expression, shining eyes and full smile would have brought Elizabeth joy. Moreover, Mary hadn't come alone. She was carrying Jesus in her womb. So, she was sparkling with warmth and life. By looking at Mary, Elizabeth somehow saw Jesus as well. By conversing with Mary, Elizabeth also spoke with him. Mary still bears Jesus. In fact, now that she's with him in paradise, he is even more intimately united to her than he was during the nine months in her womb. And so whoever approaches Mary will always find Jesus, and whoever reaches out to her will always touch her son. Although Mary was carrying the Lord in her womb, she did not arrive at Elizabeth's door to be served but to serve. Whenever Mary approaches us, it is in order to help us as well.

Mary's first visitation was to Elizabeth. In a similar way to St Thérèse of Lisieux, who said, 'I will spend my heaven doing good on earth', Mary today continues to visit millions of people. What she did once on earth she does continually now that she is in heaven. Her goal is always to help us as she helped her cousin Elizabeth. And she invariably comes to the doors of our hearts with Jesus inside her. She arrives without fanfare or fuss, so discreetly that we often don't notice she is there but we feel the effects of her presence, even if we don't recognise that she is their cause. There are times when, like Elizabeth, we too have felt something moving and kicking inside, indicating new life. These are exhilarating moments, even when we don't know how they have come to happen or why. In John's Gospel, John the Baptist says: 'The friend of the bridegroom, who stands and hears him, rejoices greatly at the bridegroom's voice. For this reason my joy has been fulfilled' (Jn.3:29). When John the Baptist was in the womb, he wasn't able to think or speak, and so he wasn't capable of putting words to what caused him to jump with delight. Understanding often only comes later. We live our lives forwards but can only understand our

38

lives backwards, as Søren Kierkegaard, the Danish religious thinker, once remarked. However, once we become aware of Mary's discreet 'visitations', our sense of joy will truly deepen, and bear fruit in wonder and gratitude.

My soul magnifies the Lord. Oh Lord, every bird has
a song to sing, and it would be a tragedy if I were not
to sing my song, not to praise you with my distinctive
voice, this voice and self you have given me. You have
given me a way of praising and a way of being that are
thoroughly my own.
Lord, I know you don't mind if my singing isn't
completely in tune. What you want is that my whole
being should praise you, whether pitch-perfect or not.
Strengthen me in my longing.
Stay with me as I struggle,
Rejoice with me in my loving.
Help me to become as attuned to you as Mary was.

CHAPTER 4

Born In Bethlehem

'Do you think that at Bethlehem Joseph forgot his
two treasures for even a moment? Everything in his
heart was centred on them. Do as he did.'
Gabrielle Bossis, *He and I*

The Son of God became the Son of Mary, and received her
cells and her flesh. His body grew inside hers, and the author of all life now depended upon Mary for his very surviv-
al. After five weeks or so, the heart of Jesus started beating.
And during those entire nine months, Jesus, like any child
in the womb, was only able to breathe with the help of Mary,
through the placenta and the umbilical cord. All during her
pregnancy, Mary carried Jesus right under her heart, and
ever after, she carried him right inside her heart.

Let's spare a thought for Joseph, however. When he dis-
covered that Mary was pregnant, he must have been dis-
traught. He had nothing to do with the conception of her
child, for he had fully respected her private vow of virginity to the Lord. Could he have imagined then, that another
man had something to do with the conception of this child?
Given the apparent evidence of someone else's involvement
with Mary, would he be able to retain his great respect for
her? Ultimately, he decided not to denounce Mary public-
ly and instead, Joseph resolved to separate from her in a
quiet and discreet way. Then an angel appeared to him in a
dream, explaining that Mary had conceived by the power of
the Holy Spirit, and that she would bear a son named Jesus
who would save his people from their sins. Joseph accepted

these words spoken to him in a dream. This acceptance is evidence of his faith. Joseph had faith because he wanted to have faith. He wanted to believe with all his heart that God would not let him down, and he wanted to believe the best about Mary.

Because of a decree that a census was to be carried out in Palestine, Joseph, who was of the house of David, had to travel to Bethlehem, the town of David. It must have been a real worry for Joseph that Mary, so advanced in her pregnancy, had to make the eighty-mile journey as well. He would have preferred to spare her such discomfort. But Mary would have seen things differently. When Joseph told her about the edict ordering all members of the house of David to register in Bethlehem, she, steeped as she was in Scripture, would have no doubt recalled the verse from the prophet Micah: 'But you, Bethlehem Ephrathah, though you are small among the clans of Judah, out of you will be born the ruler over Israel'. Bethlehem of course was the City of David, since King David was born there. During his reign, life had been good for the people of Israel, and many were hoping that God would once again choose a king of the calibre of David. Mary certainly remembered the words of the Angel Gabriel to her: 'the Lord God will give him the throne of his ancestor David' (*Lk.1:32*). Mary would have also realized that although the Roman Emperor, Caesar Augustus, seemed to be in command, issuing the order for all his subjects to be counted, he was in fact only an instrument in God's hands. It was the Father who wanted Jesus to be born in Bethlehem.

Bethlehem literally means 'house of bread' (the Hebrew *beth* means 'house of' and *lechem* is 'bread'). We cannot choose where we are born, but Christ did. He chose to be born in the house of bread. God shows his fatherliness by giving us bread – 'Give us this day our daily bread' – and so it was fitting that his only-begotten son was born in a town whose name evokes this daily and sustaining nourishment. Mary, for her part, placed Jesus in a manger. As a rule, a baby is not placed in a manger, but food is, since it is a trough from which animals are fed – interestingly, the French verb for 'to eat' is *manger*. Although Mary placed the child Jesus there from necessity, it was also as though she intuitively understood that Jesus wanted to nourish us from the moment of his birth. The birthplace of Jesus also prefigured the mystery of the Eucharist: Jesus later called himself 'the bread of life' (*Jn.6:35*), and at the Last Supper, he broke bread and gave it to the apostles, saying: 'This is my body, which is given for you' (*Lk.22:19*). Jesus wanted his house of bread, his Bethlehem, to be in our hearts. Mary understood this. She comprehended what the German mystic Angelus Silesius put into words centuries later: 'Oh, if only your heart would become a crib, God would once again become a child on this earth.'

To get from Nazareth to Bethlehem, Joseph and Mary probably headed south along the flat land at the side of the Jordan River, before turning west to climb through the hills encircling Jerusalem, and from there, on to Bethlehem. It wasn't an easy journey, and the closer they got to Jerusalem, the more uphill and downhill it was. Bethlehem was already crowded, since thousands of people from the house of David were registering for the census ordered by Augustus. Joseph searched in vain for lodgings. Men like to be providers, and Joseph would have wanted to provide the best place possible for Mary, since the time of giving birth was upon her. But one door after another of even modest houses closed in their faces. Although Joseph had relatives and acquaintances in his town of origin, none of them was willing to reach out to him and his pregnant wife. He must have been embarrassed, indignant and ashamed. Mary realised, however, that God wanted things this way. Mary was convinced that from all eternity the Father had chosen a simple stable as the birthplace for the redeemer of the world, and she guessed this was so that his son's humility and poverty would be an example for everyone. So while the Emperor Augustus, who ruled from the Atlantic in the west to the Euphrates in the east, sat in the luxury of his palace on the Palatine Hill in Rome, the real emperor was being born in an unadorned stable in the tiny town of Bethlehem.

Mary did not decide when and where Jesus was to be born. Mary did not decide *when* Jesus was to be born: this was the result of natural processes. She did not decide *where* Jesus was to be born: this was the result of a decree issued by the Roman Emperor. In other words, Mary accepted things as they were, she let them be. She didn't try to change the rules to suit herself. She didn't try to change the rules to suit herself. She didn't try to play God; she was at peace with being herself.

The prologue to St John's Gospel tells us that 'the Word became flesh and dwelt amongst us'. It was such a sublime moment that Jesus once told St Gertrude the Great that 'anyone who inclines at these words [the Word was made flesh], from gratitude and devotion, giving me thanks for having become man for his sake, I also incline to him, by a pure movement of my goodness; and I offer, from my inmost heart, all the fruit and merit of my humanity to God the Father, that the eternal beatitude of this person may be doubled.' The first person to bow in rapt adoration before this mystery, the first one to know that God truly became a human being, with flesh, bones and a beating heart was Mary.

Perhaps that night Joseph lit a small fire near the entrance to the stable to keep Mary warm. And who knows, maybe the moon, as it climbed high in the clear starry sky, spread its glow over everything inside, transforming the stones into blocks of silver, the cobwebs into delicate necklaces, and the hay into a loosely bound bundle of bright ribbons. Such a tide of silver light flooding everything in the stable would have made it appear more beautiful than even the imperial palace in Rome. Light changes everything: no wonder you hear Irish people say that when the sun shines, there is no place they would rather be than Ireland. 'The true light that gives light to everyone was coming into the world' (*Jn.1:9*). And as for the people who walked in darkness – they were about to be illuminated.

After giving birth, Mary wrapped her tiny son in swaddling clothes. The heavenly Father had no reluctance in entrusting his only-begotten son to Mary. He was happy to have Mary wrap Jesus tightly in these bands of cloth and to hold him in her arms. He was happy to see his son's complete dependence upon her. If he trusted her so much with his own son, it makes sense that he would trust her to care for us in a spiritual way as well. Were we to ask her, perhaps she might even wrap us with the very virtues and merits of her child.

The Lebanese poet Kahlil Gibran wrote: 'Your children are not your children . . . They come through you but not from you'. It can be difficult for a mother to accept this truth, because although the umbilical cord is cut soon after birth, a bond remains between mother and child that can never be fully broken. Although Mary felt this intimate bond with Jesus, she also knew that her child was not her child, in the sense that he was above all the Son of the Father. Moreover, she knew that the Son of God hadn't come on earth just to be with her. Instead, as the angel who spoke to Joseph in a dream had explained, his purpose was to 'save his people from their sins'. It's difficult to have the kind of freedom that Mary had. On the one hand, she felt an intense love for Jesus but on the other hand, she still wanted to let God be God: she was always Mary of the 'let it be', letting God be God. It would have been tempting for Mary to say to herself: 'no one else will ever really love this child as I do. He will be safer staying in my arms. I'm not going to let him go.' Instead, she probably said something to herself like this: 'perhaps no one else will ever really feel for this child as I do. But I'm not going to cling to him because of that, and I'm not going to keep him for myself, because that's not what his Father wants.'

Just after Mary gave birth to Jesus, an angel of the Lord appeared to some shepherds who were watching over their flocks, announcing the news of the birth of Jesus. The angel told the shepherds that they would find the child 'wrapped in bands of cloth and lying in a manger'. There were no neighbours or friends around to celebrate the birth of this most special of children, so God provided the choir and the chorus instead. A host of angels appeared in the sky, praising God in sublime harmony. Music filled the air, and the birth of Jesus was welcomed with a joy beyond all human joy. Being poor, the shepherds had nothing much apart from their sheep. When they were told the child was lying in the poverty of a manger, they may have brought wool to keep him warm. If any of the shepherds had a wife himself, he would have known that it can take a few days for mothers to be able to produce a supply of milk for their newborn babies, in which case he may have thought of bringing a few drops of sheep's milk for Jesus.

We're told that when the shepherds went on their way, 'Mary treasured all these things in her heart and continued to meditate upon them' (Lk.2:19). When you treasure things in your heart, you don't just think about them for five or ten minutes, you shelter them in your heart for good. What's more, you open up this inner treasure chest again and again. That's probably what Mary did, and each time she spread the many wonders in front of her mind's eye: the birth of Jesus, the help of Joseph, the stable in Bethlehem, the arrival of the shepherds, the prophecies of the Old Testament . . . And when they were laid out in front of her, she arranged them in different patterns to see how one pearl of great price might throw light on another. In fact, the original Greek word that the Gospel of Luke uses for 'treasured' actually means putting things side by side in order to compare them. Perhaps Mary placed the encounter with the local shepherds alongside the verse from Isaiah which predicted that God would come like a mild and tender shepherd, carrying the lambs in his arms, holding them close to his heart and gently leading those with young. As well as playing these events over and over in her memory and putting her experiences side by side with Scripture in order to figure out what it was all saying to her, Mary undoubtedly brought everything into God's presence as well. After all, she was literally in God's presence, physically closer to the Son of God than anyone ever was. And she knew that anything that had to do with Jesus was important, no matter how insignificant it might initially appear. That's why she took such care to meditate, ponder on and sift through everything. We can take a leaf from her book by savouring our experiences, by taking the time to be grateful for them, and by asking the light of the Holy Spirit to help us see their importance.

'After eight days, it was time to circumcise the child; and he was called Jesus, the name given by the angel before he was conceived in the womb' *(Lk.2:21)*. After the joy Mary experienced in giving birth to the word made flesh, tears of sorrow followed all too soon. I'm sure Mary must have asked herself why the precious blood of her tiny baby had to be allowed to flow only eight days after his birth. Why should he start shedding his blood on our behalf long before he could walk or talk, before he was even able to hold his head up on his own? Since it was part of the divine plan that he would one day suffer terribly on behalf of the whole human race, why not spare him suffering now? Moreover, why should the law wound the one who was its very author?

Being a woman of such tremendous compassion, she may

well have implored the Father to allow her to experience this pain in place of Jesus, begging that the flesh of her baby would be rendered immune to the cut of the knife so that it would descend upon her instead. Once she understood that the Father wanted his son to undergo this painful incision, she was more than willing to say, as she always did: 'behold the handmaid of the Lord, be it done unto me according to Thy word'.

The ritual of circumcision was also the moment when a name was given to each male child. Neither Mary nor Joseph chose the name of the divine child: the name was revealed to them. Each was told, independently of the other, the name that God had chosen. At the Annunciation, the angel Gabriel told the Virgin Mary: 'you will name him Jesus' *(Lk.1:31)*. And an angel spoke to Joseph in a dream, explaining the connection between the name and the mission: 'you are to name him Jesus, for he will save his people from their sins' *(Mt.1:21)*. Mary was aware of the power of the name 'Jesus' as no other person ever has been, or ever will be. And since this name was received at his circumcision, she knew that salvation would happen at an extremely high price to Jesus himself. On Calvary, this name became deep crimson with blood. It shone from the cross, and still shines upon anyone who calls upon it, praises it and believes in it. Mary knew there would never be another name like it, 'far above all rule and authority and power and dominion, and above every name that is named, not only in this age, but also in the age to come' *(Eph.1:21)*.

Son of the Father and Son of Mary, you are called 'Jesus'
so that we can be called children of God. Your Name is
the only name under heaven by which we can be saved.
Give us unbounded confidence in your Holy Name.
Jesus, Splendour of the Father, shine your light upon us.
Jesus, Prince of Peace, calm our anxieties. Jesus, Eternal

Wisdom, forgive our foolishness. Jesus, Author of life, give us life in abundance. Jesus, gentle and humble of heart, puncture our pride. Jesus, Courage of martyrs, give us your strength. Jesus, Son of Mary, teach us to love your mother as you do.

CHAPTER 5

Testimony In The Temple

'People say, 'I have no devotion to Our Lady...'
Well, who's talking about devotion? We're talking
about reality. You don't have devotion to reality, you
embrace it . . . I don't think I have a "devotion" to
Mary. I have something far greater, more immense,
far more beautiful.'
Catherine de Hueck Doherty

In ancient Israel, the most sacred space in the world was
the Temple in Jerusalem, because this was God's dwelling
place on earth. It was to the Temple that Mary and Joseph
brought Jesus forty days after his birth, so that he could be
consecrated to the Lord. Through this ritual, Jesus submitted
himself completely to the Law of Moses in order to fulfil it to
perfection. As part of this dedication of Jesus to the Father,
they were required to bring a sacrifice to the Temple. Instead
of a lamb, those of slender means were allowed bring
pigeons. And although Mary and Joseph brought only two
doves, in truth they also brought a lamb – the Lamb of God.

Luke's Gospel doesn't tell us anything about the religious
ceremony itself, the focus instead is on a man and woman
who came upon Jesus, Mary and Joseph while they were
in the Temple. The man was Simeon, the woman Anna. It
would not have been easy for either Simeon or Anna to
come upon Jesus, Mary and Joseph by chance. The Temple
was an enormous and complex structure, much vaster
than we imagine: it could hold up to one million people!
And this architectural wonder of white shining marble

needed to be that large to accommodate the massive influx of pilgrims three times a year. For during the festivals of Passover, Pentecost and Tabernacles, Jerusalem's population expanded to about a million people. The Temple was imposing and majestic: its walls were twenty storeys high, and there was an open space around it that was as big as five soccer fields put together. Certainly Simeon and Anna were prompted by the Spirit to be in the Temple that day but the Spirit uses natural as well as supernatural ways of operating, and according to an old tradition, Simeon and Anna already knew Mary, because she spent much of her childhood in the Temple, right up until the time she became betrothed to Joseph. According to this tradition, Simeon and especially Anna were Mary's spiritual guides. If so, they would no doubt have remembered this girl of extraordinary goodness, would have known about her betrothal to Joseph, and so would have recognised her that day. By contrast, there is no mention of any priests recognising Jesus. In fact, by highlighting how Simeon, the just man, and Anna, the prophetess, recognised and welcomed Jesus, Luke may very well be criticising the priests for failing to recognise the Saviour.

Simeon took the child Jesus in his arms, praised God and began to speak of salvation and light for the entire world. His words of praise must have brought great joy to Mary and Joseph. Immediately afterwards, however, he had words just for Mary herself, words that cast a dark shadow on that initial joy. Addressing himself only to her, Simeon spoke of division, opposition and the sword. Mary, with the intuition of a mother and of a sublime saint, had long since sensed what awaited Jesus. She was familiar with the inspired words of the prophet Isaiah: 'a man of sorrows, and acquainted with grief . . . he was wounded for our transgressions, he was bruised for our iniquities . . . and by his wounds we are healed'. Hearing things said so openly must have been chilling. Simeon's words pierced her very soul. Every mother who loves her child opens herself up to pain, the pain of seeing her child suffer. She will vicariously suffer everything her son or daughter actually undergoes. Perhaps at the prospect of so much pain ahead for her child, Mary took him back into her arms and clutched him to her heart as closely as she could. And yet through the words of Simeon she also heard a deeper call. This wasn't just the presentation of Jesus in the Temple: in some way, hard to define, this was also a 'yes' to everything that lay ahead, whatever it might involve.

At that painful moment for Mary, an elderly woman came up to greet them. Anna, like many women, had a lighter touch than Simeon and most men. Although she was a prophetess, she did not add to Mary's sadness by making harrowing references to the future; instead, her words were full of thanks and praise. Anna shared the same name as Hannah, who had presented her own son Samuel to God in the Temple many centuries beforehand.

When Hannah's son Samuel was born, Hannah went to the Temple and broke forth into a song of praise that bears many resemblances to Mary's Magnificat: 'The Lord makes poor and makes rich, he brings low, he also exalts. He raises up the poor from the dust' *(1 Sam.2:7–8)*. As for Anna, she was the daughter of Phanuel, a name which means 'Face of God'. Now, as she looked at the child that Mary was holding in her arms, Anna truly saw the face of God. Anna was of the tribe of Asher, named after the second son of the patriarch Jacob.

The word 'Asher' means blessed. Indeed, when Jacob's son Asher was born, Jacob's wife Leah said, 'Blessed am I! For the women will call me blessed' *(Gen.30:13)*. This cry of exultation is remarkably similar to something Mary said hundreds of years later in her Magnificat: 'from now on all generations shall call me blessed' *(Lk.1:48)*. As Anna contemplated Jesus and his mother Mary, she saw something strangely familiar – another Leah and another Asher – and at the same time two faces that were refreshingly new.

As well as praising God when she saw the child Jesus, Anna immediately began to share the good news, speaking about Jesus 'to all who were looking for the redemption of Jerusalem'. Meanwhile, something profound was taking place within Mary. Like Abraham, who had shown his willingness to sacrifice his son Isaac, Mary offered the life of Jesus to the Father. The difference was that although Abraham did not have to go through with his sacrifice, Mary did. Mary's offering was made at the Presentation, and would eventually be fulfilled on Calvary. In the silence of Mary's heart, something deep, beautiful and heroic was unfolding. That's because Mary lived love, and the heart of love is to give ourselves. She gave fully of herself, already, in advance, thus imitating the sacrificial love of Jesus. We could all learn from this gentle woman to give of ourselves more and more generously to God.

Despite the sorrow Mary felt at this moment, there is no suggestion that she was a sorrowful kind of person, or that she had a disheartening influence upon her son. Her sorrowful experiences did not burden her with a pessimistic outlook, and they did not make her unequal to the various challenges she had to face over the course of her life. Mary was a woman of hope. Just as Jesus would later turn water into wine at Mary's request, God seems to have given this most blessed among women the disarming grace of transforming even sorrow into joy. She needed this kind of resilience, because she was about to be completely uprooted from her country, culture and people.

Mary, help us to be generous in following Jesus. Help
us to give the best of ourselves, and not the worst.
Encourage us to give all of our hearts and not just fifty

*per cent. And to spur us on, strengthen our trust that
God will do great things through us, if only we make this
gift of ourselves. And when these great things happen,
keep us grounded: show us that it is because of God, and
not ourselves, that blessings flow through our hands.*

CHAPTER 6

Leaving To Live

'Sometimes I long for a convent cell, with the
sublime wisdom of centuries set out on bookshelves
all along the wall and a view across the cornfields
– there must be cornfields and they must wave in
the breeze – and there I would immerse myself in
the wisdom of the ages and in myself. Then I might
perhaps find peace and clarity. But that would be no
great feat. It is right here, in this very place, in the
here and the now, that I must find them.'
Etty Hillesum, *An Interrupted Life*

It was because of Jesus that Mary and Joseph had to set out
for a foreign country but before that happened, foreigners voluntarily arrived in Palestine, also because of Jesus.
These wise men or Magi made a long journey, following a
star, until it finally stopped in Bethlehem. 'On entering the
house, they saw the child with Mary his mother; and they
fell down and worshipped him. Then, opening their trea-
sure-chests, they offered him gifts of gold, frankincense and
myrrh' *(Mt.2:1,11)*. By this time, Mary and Joseph were no
longer in a stable, but in a house with the child Jesus, so the
baby must have been at least a few months old. With the
security of living in a house, they had time to gather their
energies and gain strength for whatever the Father would
next ask of them.

Notice that the Magi did not adore Mary. The Magi
worshipped Jesus, and that's because only God is worthy
of being worshipped and adored because only God is an

infinitely perfect being, and we depend upon him. They certainly would have respected Mary greatly, because they would have seen a reflection of God's goodness in her countenance and bearing. Just as she held Jesus in her arms with exquisite reverence when he was shown after his birth to the people of Israel in the form of the simple shepherds, so now she was with Jesus again, contemplating him with her adoring eyes, at the moment the people of the wider world came in the form of these wise and wealthy men. Mary must have felt great joy at the sight of the Magi and at this stirring sign that the prophetic predictions about Jesus were beginning to be fulfilled. And a great sense of gratitude for their gifts as well. Who knows, perhaps their gift of gold may have been just what she and Joseph needed to get a roof over their heads when they first arrived with Jesus in the land of Egypt.

They fled to Egypt because of the words spoken to Joseph by an angel in a dream. In one way, they were at a disadvantage starting out from Bethlehem. Joseph was a carpenter, and he needed to have the tools of his trade in order to support Jesus and Mary while they were in exile. But his implements were in Nazareth, not in Bethlehem. He wouldn't have had the money to buy new equipment, unless Mary and Joseph had not yet given away the present of gold brought to them by the wise men. However, in another way, fleeing from Bethlehem was an advantage: Bethlehem was further south than Nazareth. With Herod's troops actively searching for young male children, it would have been much more dangerous to have had to travel the additional distance from Nazareth south to Jerusalem with the little child Jesus before getting on the route to Egypt.

Mary and Joseph would have been anxious as they set out by night on their voyage into the unknown. They had no idea how the journey would unfold: how long it would take, how they would be received by the Egyptians, how they would communicate with people of a different language; where they would find a place to settle in and how they would eke out a living once they were there. They didn't even know where their next meal would come from. The closer they came to Egypt, the safer they felt from Herod's henchmen, and at the same time the more forlorn they must have been as their own country gave way to a new territory with a different faith, language and culture.

It is one thing leading a life of slender means in your own land but it's quite a different proposition being poor somewhere else. No one in Egypt knew Mary or Joseph. There was no one to welcome them when they arrived there. At the beginning, the Egyptians were suspicious of these foreigners. And Mary and Joseph looked at this new land with sad eyes, the eyes of exiles, for whom Egypt appeared barren and joyless compared to Galilee with its rolling hills, green fields and sky-blue lake.

Yet, despite the challenges and the uncertainty, Mary and Joseph did everything possible to make Jesus feel happy in this new environment. There was no moodiness, no sulky expressions and no angry exchanges. Mary did not blame Joseph for not securing a dream job in Egypt. And even though Mary became a refugee because she gave birth to Jesus, she didn't blame God for sending this child into her life.

Life was frugal, food was hard to come by and each day was a struggle. But the spirit of love and gratitude that Mary expressed in the Magnificat still reigned in her heart. Her love gave flavour to the food she ate, beauty to the simple surroundings and endowed her with a huge trust in God that no uncertainty about the future could ever dent. The following words of the American self-help author Melody Beattie are particularly apt: 'Gratitude unlocks the fullness of life. It turns what we have into enough, and more. It turns denial into acceptance, chaos to order, confusion to clarity. It can turn a meal into a feast, a house into a home, a stranger into a friend. Gratitude makes sense of our past, brings peace for today and creates a vision for tomorrow.'

Mary was grateful to God for everything, even the difficult things. The American comedian and talk show host Stephen Colbert lost his father and two brothers when he was only ten years old. They were killed in a plane crash in North Carolina. A few years ago, speaking about this traumatic event, he said: 'I love the thing that I most wish had not happened.' It's clear that he would have preferred this awful accident never to have occurred. And he certainly didn't come to terms with it the next day or the next month or the next year. As time went by, his mother's deep Catholic faith certainly helped him greatly: 'by her example I am not bitter . . . She was . . . broken, yes. Bitter, no.' But it was only at the age of thirty-five, walking down the street, that he finally knew that he himself was grateful for the loss of his father and his two brothers, despite not wanting this terrible loss to have ever taken place.

He felt guilty for being grateful, yet at the same time he couldn't deny that he felt this way. Colbert was struck by a line in one of Tolkien's letters: 'What punishments of God are not gifts?' The meaning Colbert took from Tolkien's words was that 'it would be ungrateful not to take everything with gratitude. It doesn't mean you want it. I can hold both of those ideas in my head.' He had finally come to see the gift in this agonising memory, even though the gift had initially been wrapped in funeral black.

Mary had that disarming spirit of gratitude as well, a spirit encapsulated in this challenging claim of the French Jewish mystic Simone Weil: 'Love of God is pure when joy and suffering inspire an equal degree of gratitude.' Mary spent so much time thanking God for everything that she also knew how to accept the darkest hours as a gift. And although exile in Egypt was a hard trial, an even more difficult one – much shorter, but incredibly more intense – was to unfold after they returned to the land of Israel. Mary would lose Jesus for three days, an image of three other days of future torment.

*Lord Jesus, as a little child you were forced to escape into
Egypt with Mary and Joseph. Help us to be light for
those fleeing from darkness, anchors for those tossed on
the rough seas of life, and glowing candles for
those whose hearts have grown cold.
And while you're at it, Lord, get me beyond addiction to
my self-importance, so that I may become small enough
to adore you, and big enough to reach out to others.
Help me make a leap of faith like Mary's, to believe you're
truly present, really here, and that you love me, so that
I can place myself trustingly in your hands, and
feel even a fraction as passionately about you
as you've always felt about me.*

CHAPTER 7

Tried And Tested

'Love is what remains when nothing else is left.
Deep down we all have this memory, when, after
failures, separations, words we've endured, a
certainty somehow rises up from our deepest night
like a song barely heard, the certainty that beyond
the disasters of our lives, and beyond even joy, pain,
birth and death, there exists a space that nothing
can endanger, that nothing has ever endangered,
and that never risks being destroyed –
an inviolable space, that of the love which grounds
our very being.'
Christiane Singer, *Où cours-tu? Ne sais-tu pas que
le ciel est en toi?*

It would have been quite simple to have spared Mary and
Joseph all the anguish they experienced when the twelve-
year-old Jesus went missing for three days in Jerusalem.
Had Jesus told them something like the following, there
would have been no fuss and no commotion: 'After the
Feast of Passover, I'd like to stay on for a few days to listen
to the teachers in the Temple and to put some questions
to them.' But Jesus told them nothing of the sort. At first
glance, his way of behaving comes across as insensitive. It
goes against the golden rule of treating others as we would
like to be treated, a principle Jesus himself later emphasised:
'in everything, do to others as you would have them do to
you' *(Mt.7:12)*. And we also have to keep in mind the people
he failed to tell. If you don't tell a friend who is expecting

your visit that you'll be delayed for a few hours, that's bad enough but if you fail to tell your mother that you may be held up for several days, that's much worse, because the bond of love and obligation between your mother and yourself is so much deeper. However, if we reflect upon this apparent coldness of Jesus, it may help us appreciate better the way that God acts. 'For as high as the heavens are above the earth, so high are my ways above your ways and my thoughts above your thoughts' (Isa.55:9).

Mary's three days without her son were three days of darkness. They prefigured her three days of future distress in this same city of Jerusalem, during the Passion and death of Jesus. Despite the inner turmoil she felt, Mary didn't lose her peace. She didn't become indignant or angry. How did she manage this? Perhaps the story of a recent saint can enlighten us. In 2007, when a collection of Mother Teresa of Calcutta's private correspondence was published, many Christians were taken aback to discover that this champion of the poor had suffered from a sense of God's absence that lasted almost fifty years. They found it almost impossible to reconcile this inside view of Mother Teresa's soul with the joy that her face had always radiated. How could she have appeared so at peace when she was so stricken for decades?

Fundamentally because spiritual darkness is a good thing rather than something bad. It's not the same thing as depression, which is caused by a change in brain chemistry or a traumatic experience. The dark night is different – it's God's initiative. It is God working in the person to draw them closer to himself.

Depression pulls us in on ourselves, whereas the dark night directs us toward God, the God whose absence we keenly feel, and whom we continue to long for. 'I sought him, but did not find him; I called him, but he gave no answer' (Song.5:6). While depression drags people down, a person's spirit can remain remarkably resilient in the midst of a dark night. That was the case with Mother Teresa of Calcutta, and with Mary.

St Thérèse of Lisieux, the sublime French mystic whose path of spiritual childhood was so similar to Mary's, explained what happened to Our Lady during those three days in terms of the dark night. Thérèse was convinced that Jesus was giving Mary as an example and inspiration for all who find themselves tormented by God's absence, so that they would not give up hope. Thérèse wrote: 'Now I understand the mystery of the Temple, the hidden words of my lovable King. Mother, your sweet Child wants you to be the example of the soul searching for him in the night of faith.'

It's difficult to believe in God's love during these times of anguish. Someone once said that the moment we experience the greatest gentleness on the part of a surgeon is ironically when we're bleeding under the wound inflicted by his scalpel. That's the moment he's closest to us. Something similar occurs in our relationship with God. But of course at the time itself everything appears dark; it's only later that we see the blessing.

Even though Mary went through a spiritual trial, it was thoroughly real at the same time. Although the city was steadily shrinking back to its normal size after the influx of pilgrims had swelled the population to one million inhabitants during Passover, Jerusalem was still thronged with people when she and Joseph returned there to search for Jesus. And there were so many twelve-year-old boys in town that trying to find Jesus was like trying to discover the proverbial needle in the haystack. All sorts of anxieties crossed Mary's mind. For instance, she could well have been worried that Jesus had somehow fallen into the hands of the son of Herod the Great, who had a reputation for cruelty. We know that when Mary and Joseph first returned from Egypt with the child Jesus, Joseph was afraid to enter Judaea precisely on account of this very man: 'But when he heard that Archelaus was ruling over Judaea in place of his father Herod, he was afraid to go there' *(Mt.2:22)*. Archelaus' reputation for cruelty was well-founded. Indeed before he even officially took charge, Archelaus ordered the army into the Temple of Jerusalem, where they massacred 3,000 people during the festival of Passover. This massacre took place in the same place and at the same religious festival where Mary and Joseph lost Jesus. The memory of that recent atrocity would have been stamped indelibly in their minds.

Mary was such a humble woman that she must have also asked herself if there was anything she had done which might have upset her son and made him want to go away. Whatever went through Mary's mind, she keenly felt the loss of Jesus – and although this was painful, it was also a good thing. The most worrying thing of all would be to lose God and not to be worried at this immense loss.

When Mary and Joseph eventually found Jesus, his mother couldn't help asking, 'Why did you do this to us?' After three days of searching with practically no sleep and nothing to eat, she voiced this gentlest of reproaches. But Jesus, having amazed the teachers in the Temple with his wisdom, now capped his teaching by astounding the wisest creature of all. He answered Mary's question with two questions of his own: 'why were you looking for me? Didn't you know that I'd have to be in my Father's house?' Jesus was effectively telling her that the Heavenly Father comes first. He was saying that before being the Son of Mary, he was the Son of God.

The mission Jesus received from the Father was paramount. Yet, Jesus loved Mary with a great love, and her anguish and pain had echoed in his heart during those three days. He sacrificed her to the will of the Father to show her how one day she was to sacrifice his very life to accomplish the Father's will as well.

Lord Jesus, if Mary lost you, then any of us could. As for me, I can't count the number of times I lose you each day, because I get sidetracked by so many things that don't really matter. It's so easy for me to get caught in a web of distractions. You'll have to come and find me Lord. It's not just that I can't find you: I can't even find myself! Help me to come to terms with who I really am. Maybe then I can truly begin to belong to you.

CHAPTER 8

Symphony Of Silence

'But the effect of her being on those around her
was incalculably diffusive: for the growing good
of the world is partly dependent on unhistoric acts;
and that things are not so ill with you and me
as they might have been is half owing to the
number who lived faithfully a hidden life,
and rest in unvisited tombs.'
George Eliot, *Middlemarch*

After the happy ending of finding the twelve year old
Jesus in the Temple, they returned to the quiet of Nazareth,
where Jesus remained largely unknown for many years
until he began his public ministry. Long as the hidden life
of Jesus was, we tend to forget that Mary's entire existence
was enveloped in a holy hush of silence. Certainly there
were several occasions when she made an appearance but
these momentary episodes only serve to highlight her long
term obscurity. It is said of certain people that they're 'not
backward about coming forward' but whenever Mary came
forward during the life of Jesus, she generally stayed in
the background and few people paid attention to her. For
instance, at the birth of Jesus, some lowly shepherds came
by, and when Jesus was presented in the Temple, only
Simeon and Anna noticed her. The Gospel of Luke sums up
Mary's hidden life in a single and surprising sentence: 'His
mother treasured all these things in her heart' (*Lk.2:51*). This
incredibly brief summary is surprising because it says so
little but it must be important, because it echoes a remark

made just after the shepherds pay their homage to the infant Jesus: 'Mary treasured all these words and pondered them in her heart' (*Lk.2:19*).

Mary's example teaches us the importance of cultivating an inner life. In our twittering, texting, blogging, posting, instagraming and e-mailing age, we don't give ourselves the time – or the silence – to treasure. It is so easy to distract ourselves from the wonder of our own being. Our culture bombards us with such a flood of images and noise that it is difficult to find a stillness deep enough to anchor our faith. The more time we spend online, the less time we have for real life. By devoting ourselves to virtual encounters, we miss out on real ones, and by searching for trivialities on the internet, we avoid deep thinking about what is truly important. There are certain atheists who shout strongly against Christianity but the most strident sound of all is the constant buzz of our culture that drowns out the gentle voice of God. 'And after the earthquake there was a fire, but the Lord was not in the fire. And after the fire there was the sound of a gentle whisper.' (*1 Kgs.19:12*). Most people would not even dream of shouting against God, for the simple reason that they do not even think about the question of God in the first place. There are too many other interesting things happening in their social circles, on the internet and in the world of news and entertainment. All of their psychic and emotional landscape is filled to capacity with never-ending signals from a culture that overloads them with information which fascinates today and is forgotten tomorrow. Although God is often absent from the picture, many people don't even realise he's not there.

Since God created everything, Mary knew she could find God's fingerprints in everything that existed. Many of us never get beyond the fingerprints: we remain mesmerised by the effects; for instance, the beauty of a person, and never ascend to the cause – God. We're not 'heavenly detectives' because we only pay attention to the fingerprints themselves, failing to penetrate beneath the surface level of things to the God who made them. We're at home in the visible, audible and touchable world but when it comes to the unseen world under the surface, we feel at sea and out of our depth.

Mary, the Star of the Sea, can throw us a lifebuoy. Mary's hidden life was characterised by treasuring things. Mary treasured the coming of Christ into the world, and so she renewed her thanks for it every day of her life. She was full of joyful gratitude for the message of the Angel Gabriel, for John the Baptist leaping in his mother's womb for joy, for the moment when Zechariah's tongue was freed and he uttered his canticle of thanksgiving: 'Blessed be the Lord, the God of Israel, he has visited his people and redeemed them' (*Lk.1:68*). Most of all, she gave thanks for Christ's birth itself. It happened in the most surprising surroundings of all, a poor manger, after Mary and Joseph had been turned away by the unwelcoming inhabitants of Bethlehem. Since this humble place was where God chose to be born, it taught Mary that simplicity and humility were huge blessings, while wealth could easily become a curse, hardening hearts into the poisons of power and pride.

We rarely pause to reflect on the fact that the Father wanted Mary to give birth to Jesus in poverty. God loved Mary who was full of grace and blessed among women. He certainly loved Jesus, 'the radiance of God's glory and the perfect expression of his nature' (*Heb.1:3*). And God always gives great gifts to those he loves, so by arranging for Jesus to be born in poverty, he wasn't taking something away from him, but in fact enriching him.

However, it is not the lack of money itself that makes poverty spiritually enriching. Indeed, sometimes the fact of having nothing can cause us to become obsessed with money. True poverty isn't something material; instead, it's a whole way of being that invites us to trust that God, who is the source of all goodness, will more than provide for all our needs.

Mary believed that God would provide, because she knew that he was her Saviour. She repeated over and over the words of the Magnificat: 'my spirit rejoices in God my Saviour' (*Lk.1:47*). Mary treasured the fact that God saved her, and so she always treated Jesus with the utmost reverence. She recognised that his greatness far exceeded her understanding, and realised that however much she worshipped him, she could never adore him as he deserved. Even when she held him as a tiny baby in her arms, she never forgot who Jesus truly was. We, on the other hand, often apply the same standard to our relationship with God that we apply to friendships with fellow human beings. As we get to know friends better, differences of social standing, wealth or intelligence naturally fade into the background since our common humanity far outweighs the accidental differences between us but it is not so with our relationship to God: there is always an infinite distance between God and ourselves. However many gifts God bestows upon us, we are nothing when measured against his greatness and majesty, which are both inexhaustible. Mary was always filled with loving reverence before Jesus. She treasured her Saviour, who was at the centre of her hidden life.

The saints acted as Mary did. One of the favourite words of St Ignatius of Loyola, for instance, was 'reverence' (*reverencia*). Moreover, the sense of loving surrender it denoted was so important for him that even this word alone was not sufficient to convey the intensity of what he meant. In his Contemplation of the Nativity in his *Spiritual Exercises*, for example, Ignatius urges his readers to serve Jesus, Mary and Joseph not just with *reverencia* but also with *acatamiento*, a beautiful Spanish word by which he meant a sense of awe that attracts us so much to the divine presence that we simply have to respond with love. In an entry in his *Spiritual Diary*

(14 March 1544), St Ignatius describes the 'great *acatamiento* and *reverencia*' with which he uttered the name of Jesus on his way to Mass. Pedro de Ribadeneyra, the biographer of St Ignatius, reports that Ignatius once told him that he had 'asked God to give him *acatamiento*, reverence and humility, and not to give him visitations or tears, if there were equal service to his Divine Majesty'. Ignatius also expressed his sense of reverence in external signs. Diego Laynez, one of his first companions, watched Ignatius praying on the terrace or roof of their building in Rome: 'He would stand there and take off his hat; without stirring he would fix his eyes on the heavens for a short while. Then, sinking to his knees, he would make a lowly gesture of reverence to God'.

In a sense, Mary wasn't doing anything extraordinary when she adored God. Adoration is a matter of basic courtesy when it comes to our creator: without God, we wouldn't be here, and adoration is the humble acknowledgement of this fact. To adore God is to place ourselves in God's presence, full of a deep sense of worship and love. To adore God is to recognise with gratitude that God has created us and is holding us in being right now. To adore God is to return to the very source of our lives, placing ourselves once again with trust and confidence in those loving hands from which we first came forth.

Mary knew her own littleness and God's greatness, and the almighty truly worked marvels for her. Before the infinity of God, she was next to nothing. Paradoxically, once she acknowledged this truth, she ended up unleashing enormous power. The combination of her littleness and God's greatness formed an incredibly potent mixture. For our part, there is always the temptation to rely on ourselves. We're tempted to be proud although we've nothing to be proud of – after all, everything that we are and have is a gift from God: 'What have you that you have not received?' (*1 Cor.4:7*). Whenever we lose the run of ourselves, we can bring ourselves back to earth (literally) by bowing down in adoration. Of course, it is the disposition of our mind and heart that is most important in prayer. At the same time we often forget how much bodily posture affects our heart, our feelings and our entire attitude toward God. Bowing, kneeling and full prostration are three excellent ways of expressing our sense of worship and reverence in the presence of God. Someday, when we finally step out of the shadows and darkness into the light, it will dawn on us how truly tiny we really are, and we'll be astonished and overwhelmed with gratitude at God's goodness in reaching down to us, and blessing us in so many ways. In the meantime, we can occasionally remind ourselves of God's greatness and our littleness by placing our faces on the ground and literally tasting the dust from which we're made.

The fact that Mary treasured everything connected with Jesus meant that she didn't just store these things in a refrigerated state and didn't keep them buried in her unconscious. She gave them a prominent place. We all find it easy to treasure the happy memories but something in us prefers to suppress the painful things from the past. Mary didn't just treasure some of these things in her heart but *all* of them. We, on the other hand, if we do think about the difficult moments, are tempted to feel resentment or anger when they surface in our minds. However, because Mary had surrendered herself so fully to God, the sorrowful moments did not make her sour or cynical. Instead they tempered her joy with a dignified gravitas. Because she kept her heart for God, she didn't get pulled this way and that by every passing passion. She radiated goodness, and didn't burn with curiosity. She had compassion for everyone, and didn't make rash judgments about others. She was silent about her virtues, and didn't do anything in order to be admired or praised. She was peaceful and calm, never changeable and capricious.

We, on the other hand, can lose ourselves in momentary thrills rather than surrendering ourselves to God. We want to be spontaneous but we forget that there are different kinds of spontaneous urges, and not all of them are healthy. We may make others laugh while our very slickness and superficiality can simultaneously fill us with self-loathing. The Danish philosopher Søren Kierkegaard once remarked: 'I have just now come from a party where I was its life and soul; witticisms streamed from my lips, everyone laughed and admired me, but I went away... and wanted to shoot myself.' Mary's example invites us to gently drop the emotions and thoughts that so easily kidnap our inner selves and to enter instead into the deep and calming awareness of the God who sets us free.

At some point during the hidden life of Jesus, Joseph seems to have died. Since he wasn't present at the Wedding Feast of Cana and never appeared during the public ministry of Jesus or during the Passion, it is safe to assume that he had died before the public life of Jesus began. Joseph's death must have been a painful blow for Mary. They had been through so much together, so many moments of happiness and of sorrow. They had stuck together through thick and thin, fulfilling together their remarkable mission of caring for Jesus. They had lived in Nazareth, travelled to Bethlehem, fled into Egypt and back, prayed together, eaten together, worked together, kept the feasts and made their pilgrim way to Jerusalem for the annual Feast of Passover. In order to have enough strength to cope with the distress of Joseph's death, Mary drew even closer to Jesus.

She loved and admired her husband who was 'a just man' (*Mt.1:19*). No one can give what he doesn't have, and since Joseph's mission was to protect, care for and rear the very Son of God, he must have been blessed with outstanding gifts and graces, a man 'of clean hands and pure heart' (*Ps.24:4*). A pure man, he freely accepted the vow Mary had made; a just man, he refrained from condemning Mary when appearances pressurised him to do so; a resourceful and practical man, he led them into Egypt and back; an empathetic and faithful man, he shared Mary's pain when she lost Jesus and stood steadfastly at her side until Jesus was found again; a generous man, he worked tirelessly for Jesus and Mary by the sweat of his brow; a trusting man, he did not become discouraged when he was underpaid for his labour, because he had already offered this work to the Heavenly Father in union with Jesus and Mary, confident of an infinite reward. Tradition has it that Joseph died in the arms of Jesus and with Mary at his side, and so he has become the patron of a happy and holy death, someone we're encouraged to invoke so that our death may lose its bitterness by taking place in the arms of the Lord.

In one sense, we know nothing about the hidden life of Jesus and Mary in Nazareth, and that's because we don't know *what* they were doing each day. But in another sense, we know everything about their hidden life in Nazareth, and that's because we know the *why* behind everything they did as well as *where* their hearts were. Jesus clarified the motivation of his actions more than once during his public ministry. Just as he had explained to Mary when she found him in the Temple that he was there to do the will of his Father, so also he said during his active life that 'I always do what pleases him' (*Jn.8:29*). The Letter to the Hebrews tells us that when Jesus came into the world he said: 'I have come to do your will' (*Heb.10:7*). This was his daily bread – the Father's will: 'my food is to do the will of him who sent me' (*Jn.4:34*). What about his heart? Jesus placed himself completely in the Father: 'I am in the Father' (*Jn.14:11*).

Mary, the first and best disciple of Jesus, followed his sterling example in terms of her intentions and of where she placed her heart. She knew that our intentions count most of all, and so she did everything for the glory of God. St Paul tells us that if we give away all our possessions and even deliver up our very bodies to be burned, but have not love, these apparently self-sacrificing deeds do us no good at all. (*1 Cor.13:3*). We're not going to be so much judged on what we do, but rather on the intention with which we do it. As St John of the Cross once said: 'in the evening of life, we shall be judged on love alone'. Mary said her *fiat* to all that life presented to her, and she always found her joy in fulfilling the divine will.

Mary also understood the importance of dwelling in God: 'for where your heart is, there will your treasure be also' (*Mt.6:21*). Through living in God, Mary took on the same form of God in whom she made her home, and her life was fruitful to an unheard of degree. 'If you remain in me and I in you, you will bear much fruit' (*Jn.15:5*). Mary left her own will behind, and embraced God's will instead. What does it mean for someone to do the Father's will? It means to love and serve God alone, and to love everyone else in him. It means to put God at the centre of one's life, to deliberately and intentionally make God the reason for one's existence. How does someone do God's will in practice? By turning to God before everything they do, asking first for his blessing and his help: 'Please help me to do this and to do it in the best way possible'. By being attentive to the least signs of God's voice. In this way, God's voice becomes more and more audible and is heard ever more distinctly so that the path ahead becomes increasingly clear. Mary surrendered herself to God's will, gladly abandoning everything of hers in order to find everything in a new way in God.

Although we have no written record of the life of Mary and Jesus in Nazareth, we at least know that they carried out the humdrum activities that we also perform each day: breathing, eating, sleeping, thinking, smiling, working, relaxing . . . in other words, most of their routine activities were surprisingly similar to ours. The difference was the motivation underlying these actions. We often think that in order to become holy we must radically change our external activities but in fact, however much our lives change, we will still need to breathe, eat and sleep; the key is to change the intentions with which we perform these acts and all our other daily actions.

It's a matter of giving God glory in everything we do. 'So whether you eat or drink or whatever you do, do it all for the glory of God' (1 Cor.10:31). Mary understood that it's not the action itself that counts. What gives an action value is the goal for which we act, and by doing our acts for God, we give our acts the greatest value possible. Since she regarded herself as 'the handmaid of the Lord', she put herself at God's service, and she served God by directing every thought and action to him. Whoever she helped, she helped that person as though she were helping God himself: 'Whatever you do, work at it with all your heart, as though you were working for the Lord himself, and not for people' (Col.3:23). Moreover, because Mary dwelled in God, she was completely at his disposition. Everything she did was done in God, and so she performed her actions with the same perfection with which Jesus did. How could she possibly have done things so perfectly? Because this is what Jesus commanded: 'Be perfect, therefore, as your heavenly Father is perfect' (Mt.5:48). Since Jesus commanded this, it must be possible, obviously not through our own efforts, but by virtue of God's grace, which God will happily give us if we turn to him constantly in prayer.

If, like Mary, our only concern is to do God's will, we shall make daily progress as our ego steadily dissolves: 'It is no longer I who live, but Christ lives in me' (Gal.2:20). We shall progressively take on a new way of speaking and acting: 'Whoever speaks must do so as one who speaks the very words of God; whoever serves must do so with the strength that God supplies, so that God may be glorified in all things'

(*1 Pet.4:11*). What we lose in the process is something we ultimately won't miss – our illusory, false self with its worries and tensions, its jaded habits and imprisoning patterns of response. What we gain is something that far surpasses our greatest capacities and deepest desires, a mysterious life that is 'hidden with Christ in God' (*Col.3:3*). No more of the gnawing restlessness of the surface self; instead Jesus loving the Father as he thinks, speaks and acts through us. 'For his sake I have suffered the loss of all things, and I regard them as rubbish, in order that I may gain Christ' (*Phil.3:8*). It's an exchange to be welcomed, not to be feared.

> *Lord, it seems that every second person wants to be*
> *a celebrity today, and sometimes I feel the same way*
> *myself. The idea of thirty years in silence has never really*
> *appealed to me. In fact, I find it hard to keep my mouth*
> *shut for more than five minutes. Maybe you could teach*
> *me to do a 'Joseph', to live the virtues that are expressed*
> *in the letters making up his name. To be Just, Obedient,*
> *Silent, Enduring, Prayerful and Humble. Teach me what*
> *Joseph knew – that the person I am in your eyes is what*
> *really counts, and not what others think of me.*

CHAPTER 9

Water Into Wine

'The Blessed Virgin is the spoiled child of the
Blessed Trinity. She knows no law. Everything yields
to her in heaven and on earth. The whole of heaven
gazes on her with delight. She plays before the
ravished eyes of God himself.'
Raïssa Maritain, *Journal*

One of the first things the Gospel of John tells us about
the wedding at Cana is that 'the mother of Jesus was
there' *(Jn.2:1)*. That's a huge statement in itself. It shows
us that Mary did not look down on a celebration like this
as something beneath her. She wasn't a rigid or moralising
kind of person. On the contrary, she was glad to take part in
a celebration where a young couple shared their happiness
with their loved ones, relatives and friends. Mary wasn't
out of place in this festive atmosphere. She fitted in well,
and she didn't make other people uncomfortable. And the
fact that Jesus and his disciples were invited shows that her
son was also happy to be part of this joyful celebration of a
couple's love.

We are joy for God but we don't realise it. Mary did. Because she knew she was God's joy, she had the deep reassurance of knowing that God always looked at her with delight. Just like a little girl blossoms when her father looks at
her with tenderness and love, Mary continually bloomed in
God's presence, flourishing like a palm tree, growing like a
cedar of Lebanon. She lived the joy of being God's beloved,
of being God's bride.

Mary enjoyed the wedding feast but not so mindlessly as to be oblivious to what was going on around her. In fact, it was she who noticed that the wine had run out. Seated at table, she may have seen the embarrassed looks on the faces of the waiters, and guessed that they had no more wine. She turned to Jesus in order to make sure that the celebration would continue. If Mary had been a self-righteous type of woman, she might have instead muttered to herself, 'thank God there's no more wine; this party can finally come to an end' but there was nothing holier-than-thou about her.

Not only did Mary turn to Jesus for the sake of the enjoyment of those at the wedding feast, she also brought joy to Jesus himself by the way she pointed to the lack of wine, because she didn't impose upon him. She didn't tell Jesus what she thought he should do. All she said was, 'They have no more wine'. She brought the need to Jesus – that was enough for her. She let him decide what he wanted to do, how he wanted to do it and when.

That phrase – 'they have no more wine' – can also be understood in a deeper sense, as the wine of love, happiness and joy. Mary notices when our joy runs dry. She notices when we've lost our spark, our drive and our passion. And she does the best thing possible for us: she brings our need to Christ's notice. Many of us find that in the marriage between God and ourselves that began at our baptism, something has become lukewarm or even cold. Perhaps as a result of our own mistakes, we feel that the Spirit is lacking. Or maybe we feel hurt by something someone said or did, and this has distanced us from God and weakened our hope.

Jesus replied to his mother, 'Woman, what has this to do with me? My hour has not yet come' *(Jn.2:4)*. The hour of being raised up on the cross had not yet arrived, the hour when blood and water would flow from the side of Jesus for the salvation of the world. I can't imagine anything except an adorable smile on the face of Jesus as he uttered these words. And Mary must have smiled back, as a bride smiles back at the groom who loves her. Even if this wasn't the most opportune moment – 'my hour has not yet come' – Mary knew that there is never an inopportune moment when it comes to prayer. We can always turn to God, at any time. God is always ready to listen. It doesn't matter if the time doesn't feel right. What matters is the humility, trust and perseverance of the one who prays: 'Ask and it shall be given to you; seek and you shall find; knock and the door shall be opened to you' *(Mt.7:7)*. Mary knew that when it came to Jesus, any moment was the best moment, and because Mary saw his smiling eyes and heard the gentle tone in his apparently abrupt words, she turned calmly to the servants and said, 'Do whatever he tells you'.

Why did Jesus call her 'woman' rather than 'mother'? Up until the beginning of his public ministry, Jesus had been happily subject to his mother, apart from the incident where she lost and then found him in the Temple. Once his mission started however, things were different. Now, he was at the disposal of the heavenly Father. He himself was already living the message he would preach to his followers: 'Anyone who loves his father or mother more than me is not worthy of me' *(Mt.10:37)*. This was his first miracle after gathering together his newly-called disciples, and he wanted them to know that he was subject to the will of no human being, not even that of his own mother. At the same time, by granting the request of Mary, and by bringing forward the beginning of his mission, Jesus wanted his disciples to know how powerful her intercession was, and how he would never refuse her petitions. Jesus came into the world through his mother, and he wants the world to come to him through her. Indeed, just as she gave birth to Jesus a first time in Bethlehem, so here at Cana, she gave birth a second time to him: this time she gave birth to his mission, to his new and public ministry. Even though it was, in a sense, a 'premature birth', for Jesus protested that 'my hour has not yet come'. Notice too that Mary didn't pray for herself at all: she intervened with Jesus in order to spare the newly-wedded couple from embarrassment and humiliation. That's Mary: noticing our needs before we do, full of compassion, always thinking of others and never asking anything for herself.

Being a good Jewish woman, Mary's words to the servants – 'Do whatever he tells you' – echoed the words of her people at Mount Sinai: 'everything the Lord has said, we will do' (Ex.19:8). This advice to the servants is of great significance. By uttering these simple words, Mary gave them a lesson about the importance of allowing God to be God. A different kind of mother would have taken over herself, and started ordering everyone around: 'do this first, then that . . .' but Mary simply left it at telling them to do what she herself had always been doing: God's will. Mary never wanted to do anything other than what brought joy to God. Mary's words give us the key to being everything God wants us to be: 'do whatever he tells you'. Mary invites each of us to embrace God's will at every moment.

It's one thing to note that Mary said 'do whatever he tells you'. It's another thing to remark that these words of Mary were in a sense her final testament because they are the last words of hers that the gospels ever record. That kind of observation makes us pay more attention to what Mary said at that moment. It is worth reflecting upon her words of wisdom. These profoundly important words of Mary – 'do whatever he tells you' – show that she didn't wait until her time on earth had ended to say what was most significant. She already said it during the wedding at Cana, because she already knew what was most important long before her life on earth came to a close. Mary knew what she wanted to say and what we needed to hear. And at the very inception of Jesus's ministry, she said it: 'do whatever he tells you'.

Jesus gave orders that at first seem strange. He told them

to fill six enormous jars with a stupendous amount of water. These jars were intended for ritual purification. They were used for washing and for cleansing hands and forearms before eating. But these jars were apparently empty. The jars were made of stone, and because of their size and being made of stone, they were heavy. All these physical details evoke deeper truths. Their emptiness suggests that there was something lacking in these old purification rites, that they had run dry, so to speak. The fact that they were made of stone suggests that these old habits had become hardened into inflexible rules and fossilised into dead rituals. Like the tablets Moses carried down from the mountain, and upon which were written the Ten Commandments, these jars were made of stone. But as the prophet Ezekiel said, God promised to replace our hearts of stone with hearts of flesh instead. Their heaviness suggests that the many commandments and regulations had become a sad and crushing load for people to carry. The fact that there were six jars is also significant. Six stands for imperfection, as against the number seven, which symbolises fullness, completion and perfection. Six indicates that something essential is lacking. It stands for the sadness of something which will never quite attain the fullness of life and joy that we truly desire. Yet, Jesus respected the rituals and rites of the Old Covenant. He didn't order the waiters to destroy the stone jars; he didn't refuse to make use of them. Instead he made use of these jars. By commanding the servants to fill the jars, he 'full-filled' the First Covenant.

Perhaps as well as noticing that the wine had literally run out, Mary also noticed that the old way of doing things was no longer working. It was a worn-out way of acting, based on tired and stale rules imposed from above, and on rituals that no longer spoke to people's lives. It was a world of people who had been drinking mediocre wine, and then running out of it. That was the best they could hope for. Mary saw this old world that was stagnating in its sadness. She asked Jesus to change this world completely and to inaugurate a new and joyful world. Mary took the initiative in inviting Jesus to replace these dying customs and half-hearted hopes with new wine.

In our own lives, we often feel the wine has run out, that our lives are unravelling in a downward spiral of discontent. But in fact, if we accept and welcome our own littleness and nothingness, as Mary did, it can work to our advantage. It can become an occasion for God's power to manifest itself. We can call upon the name of Jesus, as Mary did. Even if we feel we're nobodies, we can still be glad; because if we're small enough, God's power can work through us to change the world. This is not only true at a personal level but also at the wider social level. If we begin to despair at the thought that the world is getting worse and worse, and everything is falling apart, God is still God. Even if the wine does in fact run out, we can hope that this is not the last word, and that history can change for the better. Christians are called by God to let the world know that there is much better wine to come: contrary to appearances, history is not descending into unending darkness and decline. The darkness is only the prelude to a new dawn. And when we become discouraged, we need to remember Mary's words: 'Do whatever he tells you'. We need to remember not to be afraid, not to despair but to trust that by doing what God wants, all shall truly be well.

In the Gospel of John, Mary is present both at the beginning and the end of the public life of Jesus. Her loving presence therefore frames his whole ministry. Mary is at the Wedding of Cana, where the first sign of Jesus' glory is revealed in the miracle of water turned into wine. Indeed it is because of Mary's intervention that this miracle occurs, and she is the one who believes even before the miracle itself unfolds. Again, when practically all his disciples lose faith, Mary is faithfully at the foot of the cross with the faithful disciple, to bear witness to the culminating sign of Jesus's glory. Mary is lovingly present at these two watershed moments: when Jesus makes the best wine flow at Cana, and when his own blood and water flow on the cross.

Lord Jesus, your first miracle took place because of Mary. You wanted to show us how you can never refuse your mother's requests. She still has this power over your heart. Her requests are like commands to you. And thanks to your goodness, she still notices our needs. Mary, please ask Jesus to draw us closer to him, so that like you we too can be God's humble servants and joyfully surrender ourselves to the divine will.

CHAPTER 10

Standing Steadfast

'It takes so much to be a full human being that
there are very few who have the enlightenment or
the courage to pay the price... One has to abandon
altogether the search for security, and reach out
to the risk of living with both arms. One has to
embrace the world like a lover. One has to accept
pain as a condition of existence. One has to court
doubt and darkness as the cost of knowing.
One needs a will stubborn in conflict, but
apt always to total acceptance of every
consequence of living and dying.'
Morris West, *The Shoes of the Fisherman*

The most astonishing gift that Jesus received from his mother was his human heart. Not just the muscular organ that began beating while he was in Mary's womb, and faithfully kept beating throughout his life, but also his human heart as the seat of his emotions, the impetus for his compassion. When you stop to reflect, it's hard to believe than anyone could be more closely united to God than the woman who sheltered Jesus in her womb and provided him with a human body. Mary's heart wasn't her own creation: she had a heart of pure love because God gave her that kind of heart. She, in her turn, handed on this tenderest of hearts, so like God's, to her son. Mary was of course only human like the rest of us, and so there is an infinite distance between God and her but, at the same time, through the miracle of God's grace she became a glowing furnace of love, especially in the darkest moment of all – at the foot of the cross

Tradition has it that Mary met Jesus as he carried his cross to Calvary. It must have been a heart rending moment of utter grief. She may have even had difficulty recognising him since 'he was so disfigured that he hardly looked human' (*Is.52:14*). With the crowd howling and the soldiers pushing him forward, it would have been impossible to have had any real conversation but at least their glances met and in his eyes Mary saw an astonishing compassion, giving her the strength to love and forgive just as he did.

The Gospel of John tells us that Mary stood at the foot of the cross along with the wife of Clopas, Mary of Magdala and John (*Jn.19:25*). The Gospel of John doesn't actually give a name to either Mary or John: instead they are called 'his mother' and 'the disciple whom he loved' respectively. This seems a rather distant way of describing the woman who gave birth to Jesus and the disciple who was closest to him but in reality it highlights their intimacy with him, because they are both described in terms of their relationship to Jesus – 'his mother' and 'the disciple whom he loved' (the latter is the title that John the Evangelist gives himself in this Gospel, a title that in reality stands for all those beloved by God).

It's not easy to remain next to someone who is dying, especially someone who is undergoing an atrocious death. We instinctively flee from suffering, and so an especially strong love is necessary in order to stay steadfast when confronted with such pain. The love of this faithful little group was strengthened by prayer. We know that they were praying, not only because of the kind of people they were and because this was really the best way they could support Jesus in his agony but also because they were Jewish, and in Judaism standing is the natural posture for prayer. Anyone who has seen devout Jews at the Wailing Wall in Jerusalem will realise that standing is an essential element in Jewish prayer.

This was also the case at the time of Jesus, as is evident from the parable of the Pharisee and the tax collector who went up to the Temple: each man stood in prayer (*Lk.18:9–14*).

Apart from John, there were no other male disciples present – they had already fled. Even though the beloved disciple was compassionate, the absence of the other male disciples shows how distinctively feminine the gift of compassion really is. The stirring example of Mary and these women teaches us that the best way, and really the only way, to be present at the foot of the cross, is with our hearts rather than our heads.

Mary showed astounding courage to keep standing by Jesus during those hours. It is one thing to stand by a who is executed quickly but something else to remain when death is so prolonged, when the one you love has been brutally tortured and is now nailed to a cross, his life-blood steadily falling to the ground, his body weight dragging him down as he struggles to breathe under the scorching sun. And meanwhile to hear voices around you that drip with mockery and sarcasm: 'He saved others; let him save himself if he is God's Messiah, the Chosen One' (*Lk.23:35*). Yet, through it all, Mary kept her eyes fixed on Jesus; were they not, she would not have known that Jesus was referring to her (and not to one of the other Marys) when he said: 'Woman, behold your son' (*Jn.19:26*). As she looked at Jesus, Mary would have also had continually before her eyes the notice that had been fastened to the cross on Pilate's orders: 'Jesus of Nazareth, the King of the Jews' (*Jn.19:19*).

Mary, as we have already seen, was a reflective woman. She had always treasured any words related to Jesus. Perhaps the words of the Angel Gabriel came back to her as she now watched sadly at his side. 'The Lord God will give him the throne of his father David, and he will reign over Jacob's descendants forever; his kingdom will never end' (*Lk.1: 32-33*). The only throne she could see was a cross crowned with a makeshift sign proclaiming a king rejected by his own people, and the promised kingdom looked set to end all too soon with his last breath. Doubting voices probably spoke within her heart as well, insinuating that it was all a fantasy and that Jesus was a fraud. There were no cosy certainties anywhere near Golgotha. There was no feeling of faith to protect her. Mary was plunged into a darkness so pitch black that only love could survive it: 'Out of the depths I cry to you Lord' (*Ps.130*). Her sorrows had truly become as immense as the sea.

While other saints suffered by offering up their own lives, Mary suffered by offering up her son's life, a life she loved much more than her own The sight of the sufferings of Jesus plunged her heart into a deeper ocean of torment than if she had endured these agonies herself. It was her immeasurable love for Jesus that made her own martyrdom so immense. Every time Jesus uttered a groan of pain, she felt that pain in her heart. Every drop of blood that fell from his body brought tears to her eyes so that eventually she felt as though her own heart had been bled dry. 'The Mother of Christ entered into the Passion of her Son through her compassion' (St Bernard of Clairvaux).

Many of us believe we cannot be happy if we lose a loved one or good health or our job or the country in which we live. However, long before she ascended Calvary, Mary had already given up her own dreams of happiness to entrust herself to what God had in store for her: 'let it be done unto me according to your word'. This unconditional availability had become sewn into the very fabric of her being. If we limit our openness to God, we're also opening the door to sadness. For instance, if we keep telling ourselves that we cannot find joy unless we hold onto a particular someone or something in our lives, we're setting ourselves up to sink into serious misery in the future. Mary, on the other hand, was always effectively saying to herself something like this:

'Because I trust in God's goodness, I'll be able to find joy whatever loss hits me, even if I don't know how I'll adjust to it when it actually occurs.'

Mary saw a slender but sure sign of hope as she stood praying at the foot of the cross. Just when it appeared that all was going to end in complete failure, the suffering and prayer of Jesus brought about the conversion of one of the thieves hanging next to him. 'Then he said, "Jesus, remember me when you come into your kingdom." Jesus answered him, "Truly I tell you, today you will be with me in paradise."' (*Lk.23:42–43*). One act of genuine love and one act of perfect sorrow were enough to wipe out this man's shameful past.

'When Jesus saw his mother...' (*Jn.19:26*). It must have been difficult for Jesus to see Mary at all, even though she was so close to him. There was blood and dust caked on his eyes, his face was bruised and swollen and since his hands were nailed to the cross, he couldn't move a finger to help himself see. Yet at that pain-filled moment, when as Psalm 22:15 would have put it, 'my strength is dried up like pieces of broken pottery and my tongue sticks to the roof of my mouth', Jesus, on seeing his mother, uttered momentous words. 'When Jesus saw his mother and the disciple whom he loved standing next to her, he said to his mother, "Woman, behold your son." Then he said to the disciple, "Behold your mother."' (*Jn.19:26–27*).

Picture Mary standing there. She had been trying as best she could to keep all her suffering inside her own heart so that she could give Jesus only the caress of her presence and a gentle smile to console him. And now her son, whom she knew loved her with an infinite love, uttered these astonishing words as he was hanging on the cross. Now that he was about to die, he wanted to give her another son to look after her and attend to her needs. This unexpected gift from Jesus must have touched Mary to the core and filled her with a humbling sense of gratitude – there he was dying in excruciating pain, and he was not focused on his own agony but instead he was thinking of her. Such thoughtfulness and tenderness in the midst of terrible torment!

When Jesus had been presented in the Temple, the venerable old man Simeon had prophesied to Mary: 'and a sword will pierce your own soul as well' (*Lk.2:35*). The sword pierced Mary's soul in a definitive way as she stood by the cross but at that moment Jesus also invited Mary to bear fruit in a remarkable way. He invited her to become the new Eve, 'the mother of all the living' (*Gen.3:20*). It was the ultimate unfolding of the request made by Gabriel at the Annunciation. The angel had asked her to be the mother of Jesus, and now that Jesus was going to leave the earth, he was asking her to become the mother of all. The initial yes she gave at the Annunciation was still holding firm amidst this living hell, and so her motherhood became a mighty source of life, fruitful in an unprecedented way. 'Unless a grain of wheat falls into the ground and dies, it remains only a single grain; but if it dies, it bears much fruit' (*Jn.12:24*).

The hour was so solemn that the words 'Woman, behold your son' simply had to have a universal meaning: they did not only refer to Mary being placed under John's care. By entrusting his mother to John, Jesus also wanted to entrust her to each one of us in the person of John. Jesus loved his mother as no other child has ever loved a mother. And so by offering Mary to us as our mother, he was offering us more than we can imagine. He was giving us someone utterly special, and he was also asking something special of us. During his life, Jesus fulfilled the divine command 'honour your father and your mother' (*Ex.20:12*) as no one else has ever fulfilled it. Jesus was asking us to do something special: to honour Mary as he did, above all by loving her, imitating her, and respecting her. In his dying moments, Jesus expressed one of his greatest desires, which we could perhaps put into words such as the following: 'All of you, look at this woman, and see your mother in her. Love her with your heart, and turn to her in your hour of need.' There's no danger that Mary would ever manipulate our love and use it for self-centred ends. She hasn't the least trace of egoism, and her only purpose is to bring us to God.

At this most poignant of moments, Mary was totally open to loving every human being with the maternal love to which Jesus called her. Sharing in the unspeakable suffering of Jesus gave her the gift of empathising with every person in sorrow. Mary's heart, already full of grace, was able to say yes to becoming the universal mother that Jesus invited her to be. And the words of Jesus, accomplishing what he intended, gave Mary a motherhood that was not of flesh or blood, and so neither limited by time nor space but lasting forever and open to all. Despite the sorrow that filled her heart as she stood unobtrusively at the foot of the cross, Mary also felt the peace of knowing that many people, starting with the beloved disciple, would make their way more securely to God through her motherly help.

God filled Mary with such unbelievable compassion, such indescribable goodness of heart, that anyone can approach her with complete confidence, and can confide in her without the least trace of fear. Mary gives of herself completely, and so she'll never turn anyone away. God has given her such an extraordinarily gentle spirit and such ineffable sweetness, that even the most hardened sinner who turns to her is surprised to find his heart softening and turning toward God. Like a true mother, she calms troubled souls with her disarming voice, touches despairing hearts with her reassuring smile and points everyone toward the Lord, and like a good mother, every act of kindness we give or receive brings her joy, while every time we suffer, she suffers to see us suffering. If the Son of God found support in her gentle presence, we certainly shall as well. Mary made the chalice that Jesus had to drink less bitter through her loving presence, and she can do the same for us. All our sorrows will find an empathetic echo in her heart.

The gospel tells us that 'from that hour the disciple took her into his own home' (*Jn.19:27*). Like the beloved disciple, we are invited to join ourselves to Mary in such a way that she can find a permanent welcome in our hearts. We're about to see how the apostles took this invitation seriously when they gathered in prayer in the upper room of a house in Jerusalem after the Ascension of Jesus.

Lord Jesus, as I stand with Mary by your cross, I want to cry as a child. For all the times I've hurt and harmed, lied and waffled. I look back and all I see is an endless line of debris and destruction, the tsunami of my own stupidity. Maybe my tears won't touch other, but please, please, let them touch me. Enough that I really want to change. You know my fragile heart and fraught life. You know how I've floundered and failed, and how often I've mouthed pious platitudes and expelled nothing but hot air. Your goodness has been at work inside me, but I've smothered it again and again with my sins and shadows, my cowardice and indifference. I want to start something new, I want to begin to be someone different, and yet I'm afraid I'll fail as I've so often failed before. Mary, with your eyes of gentle compassion, please calm my troubled soul, and shape my shapeless self into someone who is human as well as holy, so that I can live for Jesus – and maybe even die for him as well.

CHAPTER 11

Praying At Pentecost

'The kingdom of God means the complete filling of
the entire soul of intelligent creatures with the Holy
Spirit. The Spirit bloweth where he listeth? We can
only invite him. We must not even try to invite him
in a definite and special way to visit us or anyone
else in particular, or even everybody in general;
we must just invite him purely and simply, so that
our thought of him is an invitation, a longing cry.
It is as when one is in extreme thirst, ill with thirst;
then one no longer thinks of the act of drinking in
relation to oneself, or even of the act of drinking in
a general way. One merely thinks of water, actual
water itself, but the image of water is like a cry
from our whole being.'
Simone Weil, *Waiting on God*

After Jesus had been taken up to heaven, the apostles
felt abandoned. Jesus was no longer physically present,
Jerusalem was not a friendly place, and they were only
eleven in number, now that Judas Iscariot was dead. The
memory of the traitor must have been especially painful
for them. They gathered in an upper room and prayed. The
Acts of the Apostles names the eleven apostles who were
there, and apart from them, it names only Mary, although
there were also other women disciples as well as relatives of
Jesus present in this upper room. They needed her motherly
presence close to their hearts. Interestingly, the Acts of the
Apostles specifically adds to Mary's name the title 'the

mother of Jesus' *(Acts.1:14)*. Mary knew him a longer time than anyone else; only she was his mother, and she alone, of all of them, loved and served him from before his birth. The Holy Spirit for whom they were longing was the Spirit of Mary's own son. Indeed, it was through a unique and unheard of relationship between the Holy Spirit and Mary that Jesus was born in the first place.

Just as Mary had been present at the Incarnation and during the Paschal Mystery, so she was now present as Pentecost approached. How did Mary picture God, and what can that tell us about her way of preparing for the outpouring of the Holy Spirit? The way she addressed God in her Magnificat may furnish us with helpful clues. In the Magnificat, Mary described God in various ways: as her Lord, her Saviour, the Almighty, the One whose Name was Holy, and the God of Mercy.

God was her *Lord*, the one to whom she belonged, the one to whom she gladly gave her submission and allegiance. God's lordship extended to every aspect of Mary's life. Mary did not regard God as an uncaring and distant landlord. God for her was the transcendent one who also made himself present in the history of her people and in her own story. And so she had faith that God the Holy Spirit would make himself present at Pentecost, and transform the life stories of the disciples.

God was her *Saviour*. As we saw in the first chapter, God saved Mary from the very beginning: it was as though she were 'baptised' in a special way at the moment of her conception, so that she never suffered from the effects of original sin. And because of the exceptional manner in which God had plunged her into the ocean of his grace, Mary believed that God could transform any human experience into an experience of salvation and liberation. This included the experience of the apostles. They still felt guilty and upset with themselves after their cowardly behaviour during the

Passion of Christ; Peter, their leader, felt the brokenness of a man who had denied his Lord not once but three times. Mary was certain that God could save these men from guilt, sin, brokenness and despair.

God was the *Almighty* for Mary. The angel Gabriel had told her that 'nothing will be impossible for God' *(Lk.1:37)*. It was through God's almighty power that Mary became the mother of the Messiah. And for that reason (and many others) Mary knew that God's almighty power was not exercised in an arbitrary way. Almighty yes but powerfully caring as well: neither the poverty of the stable at the time of Jesus' birth nor the struggling years of exile in Egypt, neither losing Jesus in the Temple nor losing him when he died on the cross – nothing could separate her from God's love. Mary trusted absolutely in God's absolute providence and supremacy. She knew that the weakness of the disciples would be no obstacle to the descent of the Holy Spirit, because she knew that God could transform any weakness into strength.

God's name was *holy* for Mary. As the First Letter of John expresses it: 'God is light, in him there is no darkness' *(1 Jn.1:5)*. Not for nothing do the angels repeat three times 'holy, holy, holy'. Holiness is a glorious quality of God, which shows forth his utter majesty and his incomparable uniqueness. Mary was full of awe at God, and full of reverence before his holiness. She knew that God wanted everyone to be holy, and she was well aware that the path God had opened up for her, the path of 'yes', would be a fruitful path for others also.

Perhaps as she prayed with the apostles, she reminded them of the 'yes' she had given when she was asked to become the mother of God's son. It was an invitation she had never expected. In fact, by committing herself to virginity, she had presumed that she was effectively excluding any possibility of becoming a mother, and this, allied to her humility, meant she didn't have any inkling that God would choose her as an instrument to accomplish his great work. Mary no doubt encouraged the disciples to say 'yes' to God's will also, a 'yes' full of faith and confidence, a 'yes' courageous enough to stay steady even in the face of adversity and pain, without losing that inner peace which is so important for everyone who follows Christ. In all likelihood she encouraged them to trust that God would accomplish marvellous things through them once they gave their heartfelt assent.

God was a God of *mercy* for Mary. She was absolutely certain that God had a heart that was sensitive to our pain and misery. Indeed, she knew that the pain and unfreedom of human beings caused so much 'pain' to God's heart that he went to the pain of sending his only son to relieve us. Mary would have encouraged the disciples to go beyond their own little concerns, to widen their hearts and enlarge their vision. She would have reassured them that love is stronger than death because love lasts forever, and stronger than any suffering because ultimately love wins out over everything. She would have warned them that not caring about the plight of those around them would make them undeserving of God's care. For the moment, while they were in the upper room, she urged them to help the whole world through their prayer. Later, she had a hunch that the Holy Spirit himself would empower them to go out to the four corners of the earth.

Mary must have experienced great joy as she prayed with the disciples in the upper room for the outpouring of the Holy Spirit. Since the Holy Spirit is love in person, anyone with any emotional sensitivity would relish the thought of his coming. And Mary was of course no stranger to the Holy Spirit. At the moment of the Annunciation, Mary opened herself to the Holy Spirit coming upon her. She gave her complete consent to living in the pure stream of God's love. As Pentecost approached, she helped the disciples to open themselves up to the Holy Spirit. She can help us receive the gift of the Spirit as well.

In the next chapter, we'll explore a vision where Mary herself appears to be a kind of 'spirit'. It is to be found in the final and most mysterious book of the entire Bible.

Holy Spirit, without you, I am nothing and can do nothing. Come, boundless love of the Father and the Son. Inflame me with the flame of your love. Spirit of love, consuming fire, descend upon me as you descended on the day of Pentecost upon the holy mother of Jesus and upon the first disciples. Spirit of eternal love, renew my heart, and make it like the heart of Mary, so I too can become the tabernacle of your divine presence. Love of the Holy Spirit, may I live in your divine will, and be transformed by your gifts.

CHAPTER 12

Vision Of Victory

'Hail Mary, in union with the respect with which
God the Father greeted you through the angel's *Ave*,
and by his power delivered you from every evil and
sin. Hail Mary, in union with that love with which
the Son of God gave you the light of his wisdom,
and made you a gently shining star, lighting up
heaven and earth. Hail Mary, in union with that
sweet ointment of the Holy Spirit, with which he
saturated you and made you full of grace, so that
everyone who seeks grace through you finds it.'
St Mechtilde of Hackeborn

Reading the Book of Revelation, also known as the Apoc-
alypse, is like entering a vision or a dream. It is the kind
of book that may well turn off practically-minded persons,
while simultaneously proving fascinating for those of a
more poetic inclination. All of us can get something out of
this final book of the Bible if we approach it with our poetic
'antennae'. By temporarily leaving aside our left-brain way
of thinking (the way of logic, method and analysis), and us-
ing instead our right-brain (imagination, creativity, intuition
and feeling) we may just deepen our appreciation of this
visionary text.

Chapter twelve of the Book of Revelation revolves around
a mysterious figure: 'a woman clothed with the sun'
(Rev.12:1). This woman stands for the people of God, for
Mary and for each one of us. The whole chapter is filled with
the drama of a battle between the woman and the dragon.

What kind of battle? A conflict between light and darkness: 'The light shines in the darkness, and the darkness has not overcome it' *(Jn.1:5)*.

Sometimes we wish there was no such thing as conflict. Struggle is part of existence however, and it happens at all levels of life, all the way from the simplest living organisms to the most complex. Whether we like it or not, there are key moments when each of us must take a stand. Indeed, a battle has been raging since the beginning of time. The Book of Genesis does not give us any details of the blissful state of Adam and Eve before the Fall. Instead, it plunges us right into the point where the battle began – the temptation on the part of the serpent. Decisive battles don't just happen in the distant past or in faraway countries which are at war. There is a battle underway in every human heart. Part of each one of us is like the proud, powerful and wealthy persons whose downfall Mary predicted in her song of praise, the Magnificat. There is the surface self that is focused on having things, accomplishing things and receiving the approval and even veneration of others. This false self is never secure: at any moment power, wealth and reputation can collapse – 'he has brought down the powerful from their thrones' *(Lk.1:52)*. The false self is out of touch with the true self, because it has become a master of masks and disguises, always ready to put on a face to hide its fears and neediness.

Many of us experience a constant pendulum swing from one self to another. In the course of a single day we can move from generosity (stopping to talk with a homeless man on the street and giving him spare change) to complete self-absorption (I'm surfing on my phone and don't disturb me!). The false self promises much and delivers next to nothing: after the inevitable thrill, we're left dissatisfied. The true self imparts a joy that stays, a sense of being at home with ourselves and the world and a confidence that we are blessed by God: 'the Mighty One has done great things for me'

(Lk.1:49). The false self drags us back into the past of un-healthy habits; the true self draws us forward toward a fuller life, in which our spirits, like that of Mary, rejoice in God our Saviour.

Chapter twelve of the Book of Revelation begins with the words: 'a great sign appeared in heaven' *(Rev.12:1)*. Where is this heaven? In one sense it is paradise itself; in another sense, it is much closer to us than we think. The reality is that heaven is wherever God dwells. And if we love, God dwells within us. When we pray 'Our Father who art in heaven' with our hearts, we are praying to the God who dwells at the core of our very being.

'And a war broke out in heaven' *(Rev.12:7)*. We cannot see this heaven in our hearts. And within this place of the heart that we cannot see, there is a war raging. The war isn't an obvious one: we're not so much rocked by loud explosions and heavy gunfire as we are steadily undermined by the annoying noise that always seems to be in the background of our minds and hearts. What the Book of Revelation tells us is that right in the middle of this war there is a woman, and this woman is the Church, she is Mary and she is each one of us. This woman stands for multiple realities because the Book of the Apocalyse is full of symbolism, and has layer upon layer of meaning. In the remarks that follow, I'll focus most of all on how this woman of chapter twelve relates to Mary.

The woman in this chapter is a surprisingly vulnerable person, an earthenware vessel as all human beings are. And yet she is enveloped in the radiant love of God. She is completely taken up in God, smitten with him in fact. God is protecting her, surrounding her with his exquisitely tender care, just as the Holy Spirit covered Mary with his shadow, a shadow that is paradoxically pure light. God's grace is a luminous garment that clothes Mary, the permanently graced one, the woman whom the angel Gabriel 'christened' *kecharitomene* as we saw in chapter two.

This woman has 'the moon under her feet' *(Rev.12:1)*. While the sun rules by day, the moon appears at night. This woman belongs to the sun of goodness, while the darkness of wrongdoing is beneath her. God, in his great love, kept her free from original and actual sin, because she was to be the mother of Christ, and also to show what he wanted to do for each of us: to restore what was damaged within us, to repair what was broken and to set right what had gone wrong.

We're told that her head was adorned with 'a crown of twelve stars' *(Rev.12:1)*. St John Eudes, the seventeenth century French mystic, lists twelve virtues of Mary that correspond to these twelve stars: her innocence, her simplicity, her humility, her obedience, her patience, her love of God, her love of neighbour, her freedom from worldly concerns and self-interest, her virginal purity, her eloquent silence, her gentleness and her modesty. The twelve stars also brings to mind the twelve tribes of Israel and the twelve apostles: the woman who had been given to John as a mother is also given as a mother to all those chosen by God. It is as though God confers a special authority and power upon Mary: 'at your right stands the queen in gold of Ophir' *(Ps.45:9)*.

Yet this woman is incredibly fragile as well: 'She was with child and was crying out in birth pangs, in the agony of giving birth' *(Rev.12:2)*. These birth pangs point toward Calvary, and for at least two reasons. First, because the only part of the earthly life of Jesus that the Book of Revelation deals with is the end of his life on earth, his passion and resurrection. Second, because in the Gospel of John, Jesus compared his own death to a birth, and moreover he made this comparison on the very night before he was crucified: 'When a woman is in labour, she is in pain, because her hour has come... So you have pain now; but I will see you again, and your hearts will rejoice, and no one will take your joy from you.' *(Jn.16:21–22)*. These birth pangs do not only point to the moment of Calvary itself: they also evoke Mary's continual acceptance of a suffering Messiah, from the moment he was born in poverty in Bethlehem, to the flight into Egypt, to the simple life at Nazareth, to the misunderstandings and hostility he endured during his public life, to the cross itself. All along the way, she was 'giving birth' in ever newer and deeper ways to the Lamb who was to be slain.

The Book of Revelation tells us that as the woman underwent the pains of childbirth, another sign appeared in the sky: an enormous red dragon with seven heads and ten horns (*Rev.12:3*). Who is this dragon? We're clearly told a few verses later that he is 'that ancient serpent, who is called the devil and Satan' (*Rev.12:9*). The colour red suggests anger and rage. The seven heads may represent the seven deadly sins: pride, anger, envy, greed, gluttony, lust and sloth. 'His tail swept down a third of the stars of heaven and threw them to the earth' (*Rev.12:4*). The stars may refer to those angels who followed Lucifer by rebelling against God. But since stars are matter, this detail could also refer to the dragon's disdain for anything that is material. It is not hard to guess that he would look down on human beings – made of bodies as well as souls – with complete contempt.

All during her long journey of faith, Mary was tempted. At the cross, the temptation to give way to hatred and bitterness was particularly intense. After all, she knew her son was totally blameless. She knew his trial had been a sham, and that he was being executed on the basis of trumped-up charges. Even Pontius Pilate, the Roman governor of Judaea, declared that Jesus was not guilty of the charges brought against him. Yet, despite unambiguously proclaiming Jesus's innocence, Pilate gave way to pressure from the crowd, and condemned him to one of the cruellest forms of execution. A horrible injustice was perpetrated upon Jesus. It was a devastating experience for Mary. Just as Jesus lovingly endured this terrible torment for the salvation of the world, so too Mary accepted her part of it without remonstrating or complaining. She remained standing, helping us to see that it is possible to accept suffering with patient endurance, with both courage and love. She didn't complain or rebel. Instead, her very sorrow was transformed by her love that loved to the end of love. All the while she was ridiculed as the mother of a 'wrongdoer' and despised as a woman who couldn't control her 'criminal' son. She accepted this humiliation as well.

A new kind of humanity was being born as a result of the life, passion and death of Jesus, and the dragon wanted to destroy this new creation as soon as possible, by attacking the woman when she was at her weakest. But the dragon had no idea who he was dealing with. Mary was well aware of what Saint Paul later came to realize: 'my grace is sufficient for you, for my power is made perfect in weakness' (2 Cor.12:9). Mary was full of God's grace, and so she wasn't in the least worried by her weakness. On the contrary, Mary's vulnerability was actually her strength: she always placed herself before God as the one who had nothing and who needed everything, and so God always abundantly filled her with every good thing. Many people spend a lot of time and energy identifying their strengths. Mary was happier to identify and exult in her weaknesses so that she could better magnify the Lord. Her humility humiliated the dragon more than the power of God. He expected God to be powerful, but he never expected a mere mortal to be so utterly humble. Her humility won out (and still does) over his pride.

Contrast Mary at the tree of Calvary with Adam and Eve, whose only concern at another tree was to justify themselves. When God asked Adam if he had eaten of the tree from which he was forbidden to eat, Adam responded by blaming not only Eve but also by implication God himself, remarking: 'It was the woman *you* gave to be with me' (*Gen.3:12*). When God then turned to Eve and asked her what she had done, she replied by blaming the serpent. Adam and Eve were so full of themselves at the tree that they only saw what they could get out of it. Mary, by contrast, was so full of God that her sole concern was for Jesus.

The moment of painfully giving birth doesn't just stand for Mary's continual acceptance of every phase of the self-giving life and death of Jesus. It can also stand for the moments of difficult birth in our own lives: when we awake from spiritual drowsiness, when we are taking our first faltering steps toward God, when we make our way back from hurting to helping, from cowardice to courage, and from falsehood to integrity. It can stand furthermore for the ultimate 'hour of our death', that fateful hour to which the *Hail Mary* refers, an hour in which we ask the special protection of Mary (the woman who has time – as we saw in the symbol of the moon – under her dominion).

We all have our vulnerabilities and our weak points. And an enemy who wants to attack us successfully will almost invariably target our weakest point. That's why the devil chose to tempt Jesus at the end of his forty days of fasting and prayer: he knew this would be the moment when Jesus would be most famished, exhausted and emotionally drained. That's also why he stood before the woman when she was about to give birth. Of course we'd all prefer to be attacked where we feel strongest but it rarely happens that way. In the world of sports, for instance, individuals and teams are trained to spot the weaknesses of opponents and to exploit them as ruthlessly as possible. In everyday life, just as someone can hurt us by touching a physical wound, so their remarks can hurt us in our emotionally wounded spots. We might start the day feeling calm and fully together, only suddenly to find ourselves a seething mass of anger when someone intentionally (or more often unintentionally) pushes one of our buttons. So it's worth asking ourselves what our particular weak points are. These differ from person to person. Whatever our individual weak spots are, there are also moments when all of us are likely to feel more fragile: for instance, when we're tired or drained, when we're on our own and feeling lonely, when we're upset or on edge and when we're suffering or in pain.

The woman escapes the dragon by going into the wilderness. There's a lovely line in The Book of Hosea where God says: 'I will lead her into the desert and speak to her heart' (Hos.2:14). When we're with God, we're safe. God filled Mary with grace, and drew her into the solitude of saintliness. To outward appearances, there was nothing remarkable about her. All her life she gladly embraced obscurity. She was happy to go unnoticed and be ignored. Yet all the while, inside her heart, something marvellous was unfolding, a love that mirrored the love of Jesus. Because of God's love which flooded her heart, she could not be touched by the evil of the dragon. Her Christ-like love placed her beyond his grasp, and made her the woman clothed with the sun. As for Mary herself, she hadn't the remotest idea that she was the woman clothed with the sun because her beauty was completely unselfconscious. She didn't appropriate God's gifts for herself; she didn't try to possess them and say to others 'look at me'. She wasn't concerned with gifts at all, because she only had eyes for God.

Mary was victorious in the battle between good and evil because she always looked toward God. We, on the other hand, become unsettled when we are tempted. We stop focusing on God, and we start to focus on the temptation and upon ourselves. We try to fight against it. Mary didn't get drawn into battle; she stayed with God: 'the woman fled into the wilderness, where she has a place prepared by God' (Rev.12:6). The dragon had no access to this sanctuary of love.

When we are in a good relationship with God, the evil spirit tries to unsettle us by making us anxious, frustrated, dissatisfied and sad. We shouldn't enter his playing field by engaging with the temptation or arguing with these unhelpful thoughts or promptings. If we do, we'll probably lose the battle. Instead, we should return calmly into God's presence. As the Book of Exodus puts it: 'The Lord will fight for you; you only need to be still' *(Ex.14:14)*.

Because Mary felt tiny before the immensity of God, she also felt the joy of God's loving protection. She wasn't discouraged by her littleness. On the contrary, her keen awareness of her limits actually helped her all the more to place her hope in God, and not in herself. As for the evil spirit, Mary didn't care about him at all. As far as she was concerned, he could huff and puff all he wanted but he couldn't blow her house down, because it wasn't in fact her house: it was the fortress of God's love. Mary was clothed in the sun, she was clothed in God. We find the wisdom of relegating evil to its proper, and minor, place in the Norwegian novel *Kristin Lavransdatter* by the Nobel prize winning author Sigrid Undset: 'Dragons and all other creatures that serve the Devil only seem big as long as we harbour fear within ourselves. But if a person seeks God with such earnestness and desire that he enters into his power, then the power of the Devil at once suffers such a great defeat that his instruments become small and impotent. Dragons and evil spirits shrink until they are no bigger than goblins and cats and crows.'

Mary's example teaches us that genuine joy comes from being united with the source of all true joy: God. The more we're one with God, the less we are disturbed by anxieties, fears and pains. We don't need to defend ourselves against these incursions, because God's presence itself is our defence. Even while Mary was on earth, it was as though she were already in heaven, because she was fully in God's presence, always adoring the one who filled her with light and with joy. And as her life approached its end, the light that had always shone in her heart became more and more intense. It drew her whole being upwards, as though it wanted to snatch her from the earth and draw her upwards where her spirit already soared, so that she could sing her beautiful Magnificat in gratitude to God forever and ever. Amen.

Heavenly Father, I thank you for all the gifts you have given me. Although I find it difficult to thank you for the sad moments, I want to include these as well. With the help of Our Lady, I offer you the heart of Jesus, always brimming over with gratitude, as a way of making my thanksgiving perfect and complete, and in order to make up for the times I've been ungrateful, and the times I've wrongly claimed for myself the good I've done.

Heavenly Father, you gave Mary a heart full of love, a heart 'younger than sin', and you want to give each of us a heart like that too. Whatever kind of life we've lived, whatever past we've had, however many mistakes we've made, you still love us. You want to cleanse us with the precious blood of your son. Make us open to this amazing gift, encourage us to desire it and remind us to ask you for it.

Gabriel, your messenger, told Mary that 'nothing is impossible for God'. However much we feel we've made a mess of our lives, as long as we can still draw breath, help us Father to believe that it is never too late to turn back to you. Give us confidence to believe that nothing is impossible for you and that you are more than able to make up for the opportunities we've missed and for all the time we've wasted. Amen.